A BARTHOLOMEW MAP & GUIDE

WALK HERTS & BUCKS

40 WALKS IN HERTFORDSHIRE & BUCKINGHAMSHIRE

BY DAVID PERROTT AND LAURENCE MAIN

CONTENTS

British Library Cataloguing in Publication Data
Perrott, David
    Walk Herts & Bucks.
    1. Hertfordshire visitors' guides. 2. Buckinghamshire.
    Description and travel. Guide books
    I. Title II. Main, Laurence
    914.25'804858
    ISBN 0–7028–0953–5

Published by Bartholomew, Duncan Street, Edinburgh EH9 1TA.
Printed by Bartholomew in Edinburgh, Scotland.

First edition 1990
Copyright © Bartholomew 1990.

ISBN 0 7028 0953 5

Produced for Bartholomew by
Perrott Cartographics, Darowen, Machynlleth, Powys SY20 8NS.
Typesetting by Perrott Cartographics and Litho Link, Welshpool.
Litho origination by Litho Link.

Britain's landscape is changing all the time. While every care has been taken in the preparation of this guide, the authors, Perrott Cartographics and Bartholomew accept no responsibility whatsoever for any loss, damage, injury or inconvenience sustained or caused as a result of using this guide.

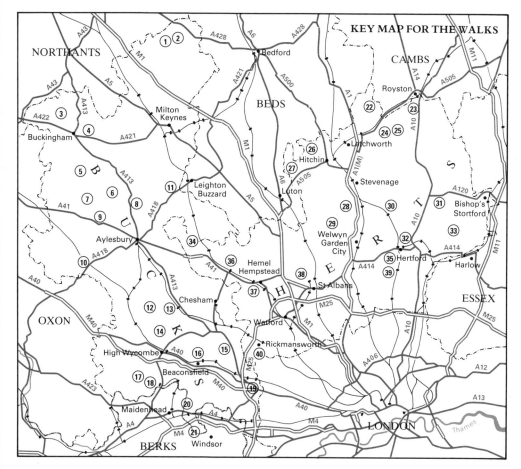

Key to maps

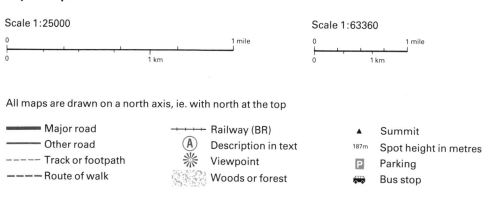

Scale 1:25000

0			1 mile
0		1 km	

Scale 1:63360

0		1 mile
0	1 km	

All maps are drawn on a north axis, ie. with north at the top

▬▬▬ Major road	┼┼┼┼ Railway (BR)	▲ Summit
─── Other road	Ⓐ Description in text	187m Spot height in metres
----- Track or footpath	❋ Viewpoint	℗ Parking
── ── Route of walk	⬚ Woods or forest	🚐 Bus stop

WALKING IN HERTFORDSHIRE AND BUCKINGHAMSHIRE

Hertfordshire and Buckinghamshire are two small, densely-populated counties on London's doorstep. It can come as a surprise, therefore, to discover just how attractive the countryside is here. Walk a few yards along one of the many footpaths and you could be in a rural paradise. In the spring there are carpets of bluebells beneath canopies of glorious beech trees. The autumnal tints of the leaves must be seen to be believed. Wonderful views can be gained from the chalk hills. The River Thames forms the southern boundary and the towpath of the Grand Union Canal can be followed right through the area.

These two counties are no cradle of British civilization, but there is the ancient route of the Icknield Way with its attendant early settlements. Despite the high level of population, the towns are all small and green fields are never far away.

Glorious walking country is often difficult to reach by public transport, but here is an area where fine countryside is easily accessible, with or without a car. Commuters travel into London from here and the public transport network created to cope with them can be used for cheap, off-peak journeys in the opposite direction. Many of the people who live and work in a relatively densely populated area such as this like to relax with a weekend walk. This has kept the footpaths open and swelled the ranks of the local Ramblers' Association and kindred bodies. The Chilterns Society has made it easier for many to enjoy this Area of Outstanding Natural Beauty by waymarking many miles of paths. Routes across cultivated fields are reinstated after ploughing, setting examples for other areas where farmers are less respectful of the law concerning rights of way. If you want to walk alone, however, come midweek when the other ramblers are in their offices.

1 HERTFORDSHIRE

The author Charles Lamb was correct when he wrote of 'Hearty, homely, loving Hertfordshire'. This is not an imposing county, despite its many grand houses occupied by the rich and famous. Everything is on a gentle, moderate scale. There are no big rivers, hills or towns. Indeed, Hertfordshire is one of the smallest of the English counties (34th of 39) but is one of the most highly populated (6th of 39, with a population of 986,000 in 1986). Somehow all these people have been accommodated without the growth of even one large town. Instead there are the original 'garden cities' of Letchworth and Welwyn Garden City, and Hatfield, Hemel Hempstead and Stevenage were expanded after the Second World War.

The small area packs in a variety of landscape. The south blends in with London at places like Rickmansworth, but towns like Hertford and St Albans have strong agricultural and rural intrusions. The gentle, rolling centre of the county is full of working farms, with attractive villages and a scatter of towns. The Chilterns, whose name is derived from the Saxon word 'chilt', meaning chalk, guard the north and the west. The Buckinghamshire border has tall beechwoods but grassland is more common towards the borders with Bedfordshire and Cambridgeshire. Watford marks the northern limit of London Clay but there are deposits of boulder clay and gravel on top of the chalk in the north-east. This is where the lumps of conglomerate known as Hertfordshire puddingstone are to be found. Barley is grown for malting in the north-east, and other cereals are grown all over the north of the county, as well as peas and beans.

Southern Hertfordshire is known as the market garden of London, and has long provided the capital with produce such as tomatoes. Now the county is being increasingly recognised as a place of recreation for the city dwellers. As the journalist and political writer William Cobbett observed: 'What pleasure grounds can equal these fields in Hertfordshire!'.

2 BUCKINGHAMSHIRE

There is no natural basis to the county of Buckinghamshire. It is an artificial creation cutting across geological features which lie generally in a series of strata running south-west to north-east. The northern and the southern ends of the county are, therefore, very different from each other.

Limestone in the north gives way to Oxford Clay futher south, the basis for the gently undulating countryside of the Claydons and Milton Keynes. Limestone outcrops are marked by villages such as Quainton. Kimmeridge Clay produces the low, rich pastures of the Vale of Aylesbury. The land rises abruptly to the chalk escarpment of the Chilterns where there are both densely wooded areas and broad, open spaces. Streams, which flow into the River Thames, have deeply eroded valleys.

The north is generally pastoral and dairying land, while the south is arable. Aylesbury, of course, is famous for rearing ducks. The forest that gave the land its fertility has been lost in the north, and beech trees have become predominant in the south, where High Wycombe is a town renowned for its furniture-making. Dutch elm disease removed one of the chief features of the Vale of Aylesbury.

Brick-making is an ancient local industry based on the extraction of an indigenous raw material – clay – but the county has found its proximity to London to be its most valuable asset and this has led to an expansion of light industry. The population is also expanding rapidly, yet there are still many unspoilt corners of rural charm. The new town of Milton Keynes has been a major cause of the influx of people (the population of Buckinghamshire rose from 476,251 in 1971 to 565,992 in 1981).

Disraeli remarked that 'there is something in the air of Bucks favourable to political knowledge and vigour'. Even excluding his own talent, he had a point. This was the county of Edmund Burke (statesman), John Wilkes (politician), John Hampden (parliamentarian and civil war leader) and the Grenvilles of Stowe (Prime Ministers 1763-5 & 1806-7). Six British prime ministers have connections with the county and five of them are buried in Buckinghamshire. The Marquess of Lansdowne held office from 1782 to 1783, followed by William Bentinck (Duke of Portland) in 1783 and from 1807 to 1809. George Grenville was the prime minister who imposed stamp duty on the American colonies when in power between 1763 and 1765. His son, William Wyndham Grenville, was prime minister from 1806 to 1807. Benjamin Disraeli was prime minister from 1874 to 1880, while the sixth was Lord John Russell, who held office between 1846 and 1852.

Powerful, influential people build imposing houses and Buckinghamshire has no shortage of these. Disraeli's home at Hughendon Manor, Stowe School (originally the home of the Grenville family), Waddesdon Manor (Baron Ferdinand de Rothschild's French Renaissance-style château), the fine example of a Tudor manor house at Dorney Court and Claydon House, which Florence Nightingale loved so much, are all passed on these walks.

Men's spirits have also been moved in this county. William Penn is buried with other great Quakers at Old Jordans, while John Milton completed *Paradise Lost* and started *Paradise Regained* nearby at Chalfont St Giles.

3 THE LITERARY TRAIL

Both Hertfordshire and Buckinghamshire have been homes to writers. George Bernard Shaw, the dramatist who wrote *St Joan*, settled in the Hertfordshire village of Ayot St Lawrence, not far from Knebworth, where Sir Edward Bulwer Lytton wrote 48 novels in as many years whilst leading a full life in politics. His dramatic comedy *Not so Bad as We Seem* was stage managed on a successful tour of the provinces by his great friend Charles Dickens.

Charles Lamb, who walked the Hertfordshire countryside near Widford, is especially remembered for the way he wrote for children. His *Tales from Shakespeare*, which he wrote together with his sister Mary, is still without equal. The great Francis Bacon, who lived near St Alban's around 1600, was more of an essayist. George Orwell kept the village stores at Wallington, Hertfordshire, whilst writing *The Road to Wigan Pier*.

Percy Bysshe Shelley lived at Marlow with his second wife, Mary, where she wrote *Frankenstein*. The poet William Cowper, who helped John Newton compile the Olney Hymnal and which includes such favourites as *Amazing Grace*, wrote good work on his own, including *The Ballad of John Gilpin*. He was born in Hertfordshire, but lived and wrote in Buckinghamshire. The statesman Benjamin Disraeli was also a novelist: *Lothair* and *Endymion* were written at Hughendon.

4 WILDLIFE

Both of these counties have an abundance of wildlife. A wide range of breeding birds are present, including most lowland species and many waterfowl. Rarities to look out for include Quail (*Coturnix coturnix*), which you may see amongst cereal crops on the calcareous soils; the Hobby (*Falco subbuteo*), a handsome small falcon restricted to southern England; Greylag Geese (*Anser anser*) on Tring Reservoirs (walk 34); and what has been called the most beautiful of all British breeding birds, Lady Amhurst's Pheasant, found on the Mentmore Estate (close to walk 11, Wing). This shy and skulking species was introduced from south-west China in 1828.

The Chiltern Hills are famous for their butterflies. Thirty of Great Britain's 58 species of butterfly can regularly be found in the north of both Buckinghamshire and Hertfordshire. The Small Blue is the smallest English butterfly with a wing span of one inch (25 mm). The eggs having been laid in June, it feeds on kidney vetch in the caterpillar stage from July onwards. In the spring it takes on the chrysalis form and emerges as a butterfly from May. Other butterflies include the Meadow Brown, the Green Hairstreak, the Grizzled Skipper and Orange Tips.

5 THE GRAND UNION CANAL

The Grand Union Canal has now become a linear walking route and a haven for wildlife. The cutting of the Grand Junction Canal (the original name of the Grand Union) is the most obvious visible relic of the industrial revolution. It was begun in 1793 to provide a more direct route between London and the Midlands than the earlier Oxford Canal. It wasn't completed until 1805, with the problem of crossing the River Ouse at Wolverton finally solved in 1811. Branches were dug to Aylesbury and Buckingham.

6 CLOTHING AND EQUIPMENT

With no mountains to climb in these two counties, there is no need to invest in lots of new clothing and equipment before enjoying these walks. These gentle green lanes and field paths are a fascinating aspect of British walking for the experienced, as well as a gentle introduction to the Great Outdoors for those who have less experience.

All of these walks can be completed in training shoes or wellingtons. Sometimes, when you come to a muddy path on a Monday morning following a night of rain and *after* the local rambling club and the horse-riders have used the path on the Sunday, you'll find wellington boots most appropriate. Some of the paths in the Chilterns are extensively used. Try walking in the less frequented areas, such as the Vale of Aylesbury, and you'll find that the clay sticking to your footwear can become very heavy! The acquisition of a good pair of walking-boots or shoes will soon become a priority. There are some excellent very light weight walking boots available now which are made of materials which are waterproof and don't require maintenance. Just wash the mud off by walking through some long, wet grass!

Even if you take care to choose a fine day for your walk, you could need protection from a shower. A good anorak with a hood is recommended, plus waterproof over-trousers. Gloves and a hat, such as a balaclava, are needed in winter, and spare clothing should always be carried. It's as important to be able to take off clothes when too hot as it is to put them on when cold, and this is easier when several thin layers of clothing are worn (for example, shorts under track-suit trousers).

A light weight rucksack is the best way of carrying things on a walk. A small one will do for a short walk, but it must have room for some food and drink, such as dried fruit, nuts or chocolate, and water. An emergency first-aid kit of patches, antiseptic cream and pain-relieving tablets should be standard equipment, along with a torch and spare batteries. Take the relevant map and a good compass and practice using them on friendly terrain.

7 RIGHTS OF WAY

These walks are along established rights of way. Please remember always to keep to the path and regard it as a privilege (as well as a right) to follow it across someone else's land; in that way we can build an atmosphere of co-operation rather than confrontation in the countryside. Some walks cross land where animals are grazed, and where dogs are not welcome. The Animals Act (1971) states that dogs considered to be a danger to livestock may be shot. The Protection of Livestock Act (1953) makes it an offence to permit a dog to worry livestock, with a maximum fine of £200. If you wish to take your dog, *keep it on a lead*.

Access to the countryside is becoming more and more vital as a means of relaxation in a hectic society. In theory, your rights are well protected by the law. In practice, some farmers get away with obstructing paths. Most people don't like to follow obstructed paths, so these become neglected and targets for extinguishment. Please report any obstructions you may find to the local highway authority, which is the respective County Council. Rights of way are now marked on the Ordnance Survey's Pathfinder maps (at the scale of 2.5 inches to one mile, or 1:25,000). Obstructions should also be reported to: The Ramblers' Association, 1/5 Wandsworth Road, London, SW8 2XX, tel 01-582 6878.

8 THE COUNTRY CODE

Enjoy the countryside and respect its life and work.
Guard against all risk of fire.
Leave gates as you find them.
Keep your dogs under proper control.
Keep to public paths across farmland.
Use gates and stiles to cross fences, hedges and walls.
Leave livestock, crops and machinery alone.
Take your litter home.

Help us to keep all water clean.
Protect wildlife, plants and trees.
Take special care on country roads.
Make no unnecessary noise.

9 USEFUL ADDRESSES

Car parking information is given for each walk. British Rail can also be used to reach the start of several of them. Others can be reached by a combination of train and bus, by London Underground, or by bus alone, but please do check such services *before setting out*. Using public transport is the rambler's way of safeguarding the countryside from having yet more roads built. It is also important to support public transport since for some it is their only means of access to the countryside. Ask at your local British Rail station for handy pocket maps and timetables and about railcards, such as the Network Card, which give reduced fares.

Both counties are fully served by a network of buses. For up to date information on routes and timetables in Buckinghamshire contact:
County Hall, Elsinore House, 2nd Floor, 43 Buckingham Street, Aylesbury, HP20 2ND, tel 0296 382000.
For bus information in Hertfordshire contact:
County Hall, Hertford, SG13 8DN, tel 0992 556765.
Both counties are covered by the Thames & Chilterns Tourist Board and have local offices:
Thames & Chilterns Tourist Board
The Mount House, Church Green, Witney, Oxon, OX8 6AZ, tel 0993 778800.
Tourist Information Centre
County Hall, Walton St., Aylesbury, Buckinghamshire, HP20 1VA, tel 0296 395000.
Tourist Information Centre
The Castle, Hertford, SG14 1HR, tel 0279 655261.
Telephone 0898 500406 for a weather forecast for Buckinghamshire.
Telephone 0898 500407 for a weather forecast for Hertfordshire.

Walk 1
WESTON UNDERWOOD
3.5 miles (5.6 km) Easy

Panoramic views across the counties of Buckinghamshire, Northamptonshire and Bedfordshire from well-maintained paths add to the enjoyment of this walk. The countryside is peaceful, and the stone villages unspoilt. William Cowper, the poet, lived here between 1786 and 1795 when the predominant cottage industry was lacemaking.

4 *At the top of the lane, turn right along the waymarked bridleway.*

5 *Turn right down a track.*

6 *When another track joins yours from the left, turn sharply left along it to reach The Alcove. Retrace your steps to the junction and go ahead down to Weston Underwood.*

The Alcove (C)

Northend Farm

(B)

Church

Ravenstone

The Wilderness

(D) Zoological Park

Weston Underwood (A)

P

1 *Start from The Cowper's Oak public house in Weston Underwood, which is 2 miles (3.2 km) west of the A509 at Olney. The bus stop is nearby, and cars can be considerably parked in Weston Underwood's High Street. With your back to The Cowper's Oak, turn left to the end of Wood Lane. Turn left up this lane but soon leave it to veer left across a stile and along a waymarked fieldpath.*

3 *Continue to a waymarked gap in the far corner of the next field and walk with the hedge on your right to a footbridge. Go ahead to reach the road at Ravenstone. Bear right to the church and go up the lane.*

2 *Cross a stile in the hedge ahead and bear right towards another waymarked stile at the top of this long, narrow, field. Go ahead with a hedge on your right to another stile. Continue across the next field, veering slightly left to a waymarked stile in the hedge.*

A Weston Underwood's High Street is remarkably tidy. The village has won numerous awards for being the best-kept in Buckinghamshire. Look out for the base of the medieval market cross opposite the end of Wood Lane.

B Ravenstone is another attractive village, with a local thatcher who maintains many of the roofs. The church dates from the 11th century and a medieval priory was situated to the north of it from about 1255 to its dissolution in 1524. Beside this site and nearer the road are some 17th-century almshouses.

C The Alcove is the stone temple, built in 1753, which became the favourite writing place of William Cowper. His most celebrated poem, 'The Task', was written here and a plaque on the wall of The Alcove shows a short section of it. Cowper lived at Weston Lodge. He wrote on one of the back bedroom window shutters before moving on to East Dereham:

'Farewell, dear scenes, for ever closed to me,
Oh, for what sorrows must I now exchange ye!'.

D Weston Underwood has a Zoological Park. Flamingoes now live where William Cowper used to ramble.

Walk 2
OLNEY
2.5 miles (4 km) Easy

Olney is in the far north of Buckinghamshire where the villages begin to resemble those of Northamptonshire, with their more liberal use of stone and tall church spires. Olney church has an impressive spire, which is very rare in Buckinghamshire. There are many charming old courts, access to which is by cobbled alleys.

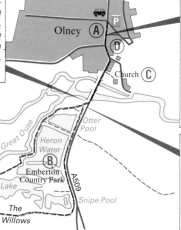

2 *Go down a path on your right after the second bridge, passing a third flood bridge on your left. Turn right along a metalled track and follow this all the way around Emberton Country Park, keeping the lakes on your left.*

1 *Start from The Bull, facing the Market Square in Olney. Buses stop here, while there is a car park in Market Square, which is on the A509.*
With your back to The Bull, notice the delicatessan on your left (the start of the pancake race). Turn right along the A509 and over two bridges spanning the River Great Ouse.

3 *Leave the metalled track where you joined it, passing the flood bridge on your right to reach the road. Walk back to the start, but divert left to visit the church and, back at the Market Square, the museum to William Cowper and John Newton.*

A Look for a small plaque on the wall of the delicatessen shop, marking the start of the famous Olney Pancake Race. This custom is said to have survived since 1455, when a housewife rushed to church that Shrove Tuesday with pancake and frying-pan still in her hand, having been caught in mid-pancake when the Shriving bell rang. A pancake race has been held in Olney nearly every Shrove Tuesday since (there was a gap from 1939 to 1948). The race is only for Olney residents, who must wear aprons and headcovering. Pancakes are fried at 11.30 and tossing starts at 11.45. Then the pancakes must be tossed twice during the course of the race plus a final toss in the churchyard.

The Shriving Service follows at noon, with frying-pans around the font. The 'Olney hymns' are sung, and there is a pancake party later. Recently, Olney has competed with the town of Liberal in Kansas for the Transatlantic Pancake Trophy.

B Emberton Country Park has been created from old gravel quarries.

C The Church of SS Peter and Paul has a medieval tower with a spire over 180 ft (54m) high. The curate in charge from 1764 to 1780 was John Newton. Together with the poet William Cowper, he produced such well-known hymns as *Amazing Grace, Glorious things of*

Thee are spoken, How sweet the name of Jesu sounds, God moves in a mysterious way and *O, for a closer walk with God.* Newton's own life story is very romantic. He disobeyed his father by staying in England with his 14-year-old sweetheart Mary Catlett when he should have been managing a sugar-plantation in the West Indies. Press-ganged into the Royal Navy, he was subsequently discharged and joined up with a slave-trader. The whole story of this and his eventual marriage to Mary is in his diary, which can be seen at the museum (see below).

D William Cowper's home is now a museum, open Tue – Sat and Bank Hol. Mons 10 – 12 and 2 – 5.

9

Walk 3
STOWE PARK
5.3 miles (8.5 km) Easy

0 _____ 1 mile

0 _____ 1 km

The school summer holidays are a good time time to undertake this walk. From late July until mid September it is possible to wander in the grounds and, for a fee, to view part of the house and the park where 'Capability' Brown became head gardener and clerk of works in 1741. If you'd rather sample the atmosphere of a public school, a Saturday in May will let you see the cricket.

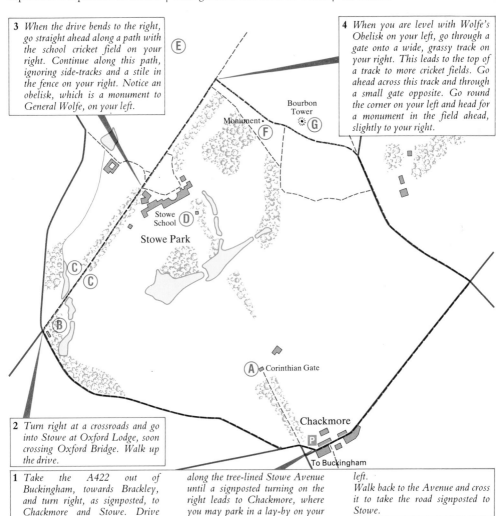

3 *When the drive bends to the right, go straight ahead along a path with the school cricket field on your right. Continue along this path, ignoring side-tracks and a stile in the fence on your right. Notice an obelisk, which is a monument to General Wolfe, on your left.*

4 *When you are level with Wolfe's Obelisk on your left, go through a gate onto a wide, grassy track on your right. This leads to the top of a track to more cricket fields. Go ahead across this track and through a small gate opposite. Go round the corner on your left and head for a monument in the field ahead, slightly to your right.*

Bourbon Tower

Monument

Stowe School

Stowe Park

Corinthian Gate

Chackmore

2 *Turn right at a crossroads and go into Stowe at Oxford Lodge, soon crossing Oxford Bridge. Walk up the drive.*

To Buckingham

1 *Take the A422 out of Buckingham, towards Brackley, and turn right, as signposted, to Chackmore and Stowe. Drive along the tree-lined Stowe Avenue until a signposted turning on the right leads to Chackmore, where you may park in a lay-by on your left.*
Walk back to the Avenue and cross it to take the road signposted to Stowe.

Over

6 *Reach a lane and turn right along it towards Stowe Castle, which is a folly. Ignore the signposted path after it, as it is obstructed. Carry on to a crossroads, where you turn right back to Chackmore.*

5 *Check that the monument is to the Duke of Buckingham and Chandos (you are off course if it isn't!). Look ahead to see the Bourbon Tower (not to be confused with the tower of the Cobham monument behind you, on your right). Aim just to the right of the Bourbon Tower ahead. Go through a gate and continue with a hedge on your right.*

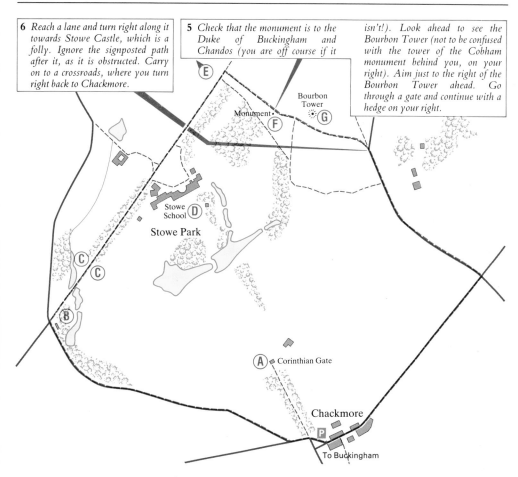

A Look up the Stowe Avenue to see the Corinthian Gate. It was designed by Thomas Pitt in 1765.

B Oxford Lodge was originally intended for another location. It was erected here in 1760.

C The Boycott Pavilions, on either side of the drive, were designed by Gibbs in 1728. Giambattista Borra altered them in 1758.

D Stowe School has resided in these palatial surroundings since 1923, when there was a huge demand for places at a top-class public school, of the rank of Eton.

E This obelisk was erected in 1759 to commemorate General Wolfe.

F The Duke of Buckingham and Chandos' Monument.

G The Bourbon Tower.

11

THORNBOROUGH
4.8 miles (7.7 km) Easy

0 _____ 1 mile
0 _____ 1 km

Clear waymarking helps make this route an enjoyable walk past features of interest for historians and nature lovers. Set in a quiet, rural part of Buckinghamshire, near the attractive village of Thornborough and within reach of the town of Buckingham (which has a frequent bus service) the walk has something for everybody. Although there are no real climbs, the views are extensive.

5 Turn right along the path going away from the footbridge into the trees. Go ahead across meadowland over two small footbridges to a third, preceded by a stile.

4 When you meet a gate ahead, go through it. Pass a pumping station on your left and then walk with a reservoir across the fence on your left. Go ahead over a stile to walk beside the old canal. Cross a footbridge over a stream and go on to where a footbridge crosses the canal on your left. **Do not cross!**

3 Cross the track, ignoring the bridge on your right. Instead, go across the river by the footbridge a little further along. Bear right to a stile beside a gate and cross the track again to go ahead along the signposted footpath opposite, with a fence on your left.

2 Walk with a fence on your right to a stile in the corner ahead. Turn right to cross it, then turn left immediately to cross another stile and veer very slightly right to a stile in the fence ahead. Maintain this direction to reach a stile giving access to a footbridge in the hedge ahead. Continue to another stile leading to a footbridge in the next hedge. Go across it to a track.

6 Turn left after crossing the third footbridge. Walk with the River Great Ouse on your right.

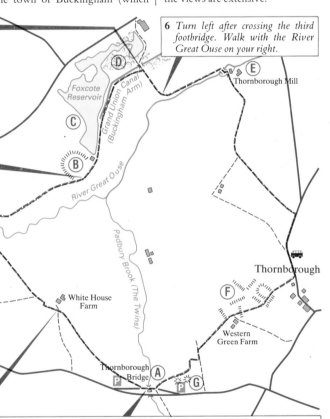

1 Start from Thornborough Bridge on the A421, 2 miles (3.2 km) east of Buckingham. Cars can be parked on the slip road on either side of this bridge. The no. 32 bus between Milton Keynes and Oxford serves the village of Thornborough and Buckingham.

Start walking from the western, Buckingham, side of the bridge. With your back to the river, bear right over a stile to follow the signposted footpath. Go ahead to a gate in the top corner and continue to a stile just to the left of a farm, ignoring the farm track.

Over

0   1 mile

0   1 km

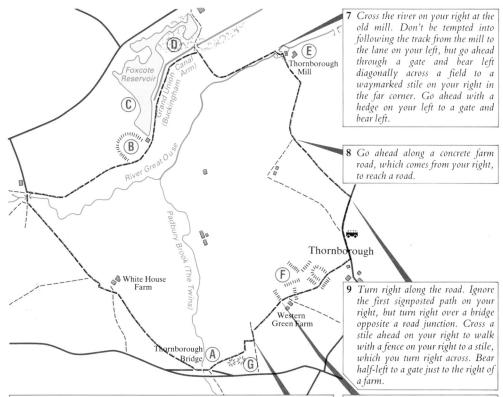

7 *Cross the river on your right at the old mill. Don't be tempted into following the track from the mill to the lane on your left, but go ahead through a gate and bear left diagonally across a field to a waymarked stile on your right in the far corner. Go ahead with a hedge on your left to a gate and bear left.*

8 *Go ahead along a concrete farm road, which comes from your right, to reach a road.*

9 *Turn right along the road. Ignore the first signposted path on your right, but turn right over a bridge opposite a road junction. Cross a stile ahead on your right to walk with a fence on your right to a stile, which you turn right across. Bear half-left to a gate just to the right of a farm.*

11 *Turn right over a waymarked stile and bear left to two distinctive mounds. Bear right to pass these on your left and reach a stile in the corner on your left. Cross this back to the start.*

10 *Continue with a hedge on your left to a gate giving access to a farm lane. Go left along this.*

A Thornborough Bridge dates from the 14th century.

B An old iron axe was found in the Iron Age enclosure (300 BC) which can be traced on your left.

C Foxcote Reservoir is a nature reserve with restricted access.

D Your path goes through the Buckinghamshire Canal Nature Reserve. This arm of the Grand Union Canal was opened in 1801.

E This mill was working up to the Second World War. Its history stretches back to the Domesday Book, when eels were trapped here. An old millstone can be seen.

F This is an example of a 'lost' village. A thriving medieval settlement here was deserted by the 17th century as a result of the enclosing of land for sheep.

G The two distinctive mounds are of the Roman period. Roman roads met near here, while a Romano-Celtic temple once stood nearby.

CLAYDON HOUSE
4 miles (6.4 km) Easy, but can be muddy

0 _____ 1 mile
0 _____ 1 km

Claydon House is most famous for its lavishly decorated interior, so you won't be welcome in muddy walking-boots. With this requirement in mind, the walk from the start to the house is along a well- surfaced path and the road.

4 *After passing the house, turn right through a kissing-gate. If you intend visiting the house, it is on your right. Otherwise, bear left to walk down the drive to a road, where you turn right to walk through Middle Claydon. When you come to a cemetery on your right, look for a stile in its far corner and turn right after it to walk with the hedge on your left to a footbridge ahead.*

5 *The footbridge leads to a farm track, which you follow with a hedge on your right. Go ahead when the track ends after woodland on your right. When the hedge on your right ends, go ahead across a field to two gates in the far left corner. Take the right hand gate to continue with a hedge on your left to a small gate ahead. Cross a field to a road and turn right back into East Claydon.*

1 *Start from St Mary's church in East Claydon, which is 3 miles (4.8 km) south-west of the A413 at Winslow. The church is at the end of a No Through Road, where cars can usually be parked. Buses run between East Claydon and Aylesbury at infrequent intervals. With your back to the church entrance, bear left to take the footpath past the Old Rectory to a minor road.*

To Winslow

Claydon Park

Middle Claydon

East Claydon

Claydon House

P

South Lodge

Ⓐ

Ⓑ

Botolph Claydon

3 *Turn right into Claydon Park at the South Lodge (it is a public bridleway despite the 'private road' notice). Bear left to follow the bridleway through a gate and continue to walk past Claydon House on your right. (If you plan to visit the house, fork right along the road from the South Lodge if the public bridleway going left to the house is likely to be muddy.) Notice the lakes on your left and the church on your right.*

2 *Bear left along the footpath which runs parallel to the road into the village of Botolph Claydon. Turn right at the junction to follow the road towards Middle Claydon. Walk carefully along this road for nearly 1 mile (1.6 km).*

A Notice the clock tower, built in 1913. It has a face on each side as it marks the boundary between the communities of East Claydon and Botolph Claydon. The parish church is in East Claydon – the large public library, built and stocked by the Verney family, is in Botolph Claydon.

Over

Claydon House

B Claydon House is in the care of the National Trust and is open Easter Mon – Oct. Wed – Sun. Teas are served in the stable block, so there is no need to enter the house for refreshments. An opportunity to see the inside of Claydon House is not to be missed, however. Its setting in pleasant parkland with landscaped lakes is secondary to its astounding interior decorated by Luke Lightfoot, a carver of genius.

Sir Ralph Verney was so extravagant and single-minded with the building of his new house between 1754 and 1782 that it ruined him financially and most of its contents had to be sold in 1783. Two-thirds of the great west front, overlooking the lakes, was also unfinished and was demolished in 1792, leaving the present west wing as a token. Lightfoot's North Hall and Chinese Room, and Rose's Saloon and Staircase,

remain as magnificent examples of Georgian interiors. Florence Nightingale, whose sister Parthenope married Sir Harry Verney, was a frequent visitor. Perhaps she knew of the ghost of old Sir Edmund Verney. A loyal supporter of his king, he became Charles I's standard bearer in the civil war and died at the Battle of Edgehill. His body was hacked to pieces, but his hand was found – still clutching the royal standard.

Walk 6

NORTH MARSTON

4.3 miles (6.9 km) Easy, but can be muddy

This is a rewarding walk across the heavy clay of Aylesbury Vale, where pilgrims once trod. North Marston was so great and lucrative a place of pilgrimage in the 14th and 15th centuries that its famous shrine was removed to Windsor in 1478 in an attempt to divert trade to where the authorities preferred to have it. Its holy well has been preserved, however, while the church was to benefit indirectly from a miser, thanks to Queen Victoria (see below). The waymarking of these paths is excellent.

A St Mary's church, North Marston, once contained the bones of Sir John Schorne. Renowned for his extreme piety, he was the rector here between 1290 and 1314. During this time he blessed the village well, which is naturally rich in iron, or chalybeate. This gave it healing properties and the sick travelled to it from far and wide. The rector was said to have caught the devil in a boot, giving rise to the rhyme: 'Sir John Schorne, Gentleman born, Kicked the devil into a boot'. Although never officially canonized, Sir John's reputation and his bones attracted pilgrims in increasing numbers until 1481, when this shrine was said to have been the third most popular place of pilgrimage in England, after Canterbury and Walsingham. The flow of pilgrims brought great wealth to the parish and this made the Dean of Windsor so full of envy that he obtained the pope's permission to remove the shrine containing Sir John's bones to St George's Chapel, Windsor. Following this, the pilgrims visited neither North Marston nor Windsor.

Much later, it was Queen Victoria who was to give North Marston back a little wealth. It relates to the strange tale of John Camden Neild. Born in 1780, he was an eccentric miser, the son of James Neild, who made his fortune as a goldsmith, invested in property in Buckinghamshire and devoted the last 40 years of his life to the reform of prisons. Despite his philanthropy, he had harshly driven his elder son to an early death and John inherited all his fortune at the age of 34. With estates worth £250,000 he chose to live in mean rooms without a bed and to wear old boots and clothes. He was a particularly hard and selfish landlord and made it his practice to visit his tenants to get free meals. He saved money by walking all the way from his home in London to collect the rents. Many tales of his meanness have survived. He once found the road so deeply flooded that he had to offer a tall labourer a penny to carry him a distance. Such was his notoriety that the labourer knew to claim his wage halfway across, in case the miser objected to paying on the other side. It was his duty to keep the church in a good state of repair, but he re-roofed it in calico rather than lead as this 'would see him out'. To ensure that the workmen gave value for money, he sat on the roof of the church with them. He increased the fortune inherited from his father to £500,000 before his death in 1852.

His will was a national sensation, for he left his entire fortune to 'her most Gracious Majesty Queen Victoria'. The queen had the calico on the roof of North Marston church replaced with lead, restored its chancel, inserted a stained glass memorial window to the miser and bought herself Balmoral.

B Marstonfields Farm is an example of conservation linked with modern farming. Relatively few hedgerows have been grubbed out here and the traditional skills of hedge-laying are encouraged. Kestrels and owls have also been encouraged by the provision of nest boxes. With the loss of many elms to disease, the dominant trees are oak, ash and willow and new plantations of broadleaved trees are growing. Wild flowers have survived here because the traditional pastures have not been sprayed with herbicide or received any artificial fertiliser. Apart from some 70 species of birds, you may see bats, squirrels, badgers and moles. The insect life is also rich.

C The holy well that Sir John Schorne blessed, and which pilgrims visited, now has a cover and a pump.

Over

0   1 mile

0   1 km

3 Go ahead through a gate and across a field to go through a waymarked gate. Walk ahead with the hedge now on your left to go through a gateway in the corner. Continue with a fence on your left to pass through a gate ahead and proceed with a hedge now on your right to a road.

2 Pass Marstonfields Farm on your left and follow the waymarked path through a gate to a field. Veer left to a gap in the hedge across the field. Go ahead with a hedge on your right.

1 Start from St Mary's church, North Marston, which is 2.5 miles (4 km) west of the A413 at Whitchurch. Cars can be parked considerably in the village, while buses between Aylesbury and Winslow stop at The Bell in the High Street.
Go north-east from the church, along a lane waymarked Swans Way. Fork right after passing the church on your left to Townsend leading to Marstonfields Road. Keep to this lane as it bends left, ignoring signposted paths off it.

To Winslow

Ⓑ Marstonfields Farm

North Marston

P

Church
Ⓐ

Well
Ⓒ

4 Turn right along the road until it bends left. Go right here along a signposted bridleway, soon turning right through a waymarked gate at the first corner. Turn left immediately to walk with a hedge on your left.

5 Go ahead through a small gate and continue across a field to go through a waymarked gateway in the hedge ahead. Continue (veering very slightly left) via a small gate in the next hedgerow.

6 Notice a stile in the fence on your left. Turn right here towards a footbridge. Cross this and walk ahead through a gap in the hedge ahead. Continue over a stile in the next hedge.

7 Go ahead across a private farm track and continue over a footbridge. Aim for the far left corner, where a stile in the hedge on your right leads to another stile just across the corner of the next field. Maintain your direction across the next field to rejoin your outward track.

8 Retrace your steps to St Mary's church, North Marston. Continue past the church on your right, however, to reach Schorne Lane. Go down Schorne Lane, past a Methodist church on your left, to see the holy well, now covered and with a pump standing beside it. Return to St Mary's church.

QUAINTON

4.5 miles (7.2 km) Moderate

0						1 mile
0				1 km		

Hills with panoramic views do exist in Buckinghamshire, north of Aylesbury, as this walk proves. It follows a small part of the waymarked 35 mile long Ridgeway to Milton Keynes North Bucks Way, over the 624 ft (190 m) Quainton Hill. Quainton's windmill is an outstanding landmark now being lovingly restored.

5 Turn right along the lane to North Marston. This is a gated lane, which you follow until the North Bucks Way footpath route is signposted on your right. Cross a stile and follow the direction of the waymark arrows south to the top of Quainton Hill.

4 Go ahead to a gate and continue to a willow tree. Veer slightly right to a fenced track and turn left along it to a road. Turn right to a road junction.

3 Go ahead through the metal gate, and veer left across this field to a footbridge. Continue with the hedge on your left over another footbridge and on to a gate ahead.

2 Go ahead through small gates, then bend left with the path. Turn right to pass gardens on your left and go ahead across a stile. Veer left towards a gate in the far corner. Go through it and turn right immediately.

6 Go through a gate and veer right, as indicated by the North Bucks Way arrow (ignoring the Swans Way, which goes straight ahead to the radio mast). Cross a stile in the far right corner and follow the well-defined path down to Quainton and its distinctive windmill. A waymarked stile ahead leads to a narrow path to the road, where you turn left back to The Green.

1 Start from The Green at Quainton, which is 2.5 miles (4 km) north of the A41 at Waddesdon. Cars can park by The Green, while buses between Aylesbury and Quainton stop at The George & Dragon.
Go to the old Cross at the top of The Green. Notice the tall windmill behind it. With your back to the windmill, turn right along Upper Street. Ignore the first signposted footpath (North Bucks Way) on your right. Turn right up the second signposted footpath. It takes the narrow, hedged, path on your left 30 yards (27 m) ahead.

A Quainton has a fine old market cross at the top of its Green. The windmill behind it is 65 feet (20 m) high and was built in 1830. It is open on Sunday mornings.

B Notice the dismantled railway on your left. Quainton is still a railway centre with preserved locomotives exhibited at the old Quainton Road Station.

C Evidence of a medieval village can be seen at Fulbrook Farm.

D The pits and mounds mark long abandoned stone quarries.

Walk 8
WHITCHURCH

4.3 miles (6.9 km) Easy, but can be muddy

There are splendid views from the ridge at Whitchurch. The artist Rex Whistler once lived here and he captured the scene in his famous painting 'The Vale from Whitchurch'. The village was once a town, with a market charter granted in 1245. The buildings retain a sense of history, but Cromwell finished off the castle.

2 *Go ahead past the old castle mound on your right, descending to a gate. Continue near a hedge on the left. Turn left over a footbridge and veer right to a gateway in the next hedge. Maintain your direction across three more fields.*

1 *Start at the northern end of the High Street in Whitchurch, at its junction with Market Hill. Whitchurch High Street forms part of the A413 between Aylesbury and Winslow; buses run here from both places. Cars can be parked at the Aylesbury (southern) end of the High Street.*
Go along Market Hill until you reach a fork, where you go left along Castle Lane. Turn left over a signposted stile.

6 *Keep the hedge on your right as you go ahead, uphill, across three fields. Cross a stile into a fourth field and continue with a hedge on your right to a gate. Go through it to reach a lane, where you turn left back to the A413. If you came by bus, there is a bus stop here. If you wish to go back to the start, turn right up the village.*

Castle

A

Whitchurch

P

3 *Veer left across the fourth field, cross a private track and go ahead through a gate. Continue to reach the road at a stile in the hedge on the left. Cross the A413 with care and turn right along the pavement to reach Hardwick. Take the left turn into the village, carrying on downhill past the village green. When the road goes right, keep ahead along the signposted footpath, which is a clear farm track.*

Hardwick

4 *Follow the farm track along the left-hand side of three fields, then on the right-hand side of a fourth field. When the track goes right, keep ahead to reach a footbridge.* **Do not cross this!**

5 *Now turn around, with the bridge at your back. Go ahead, veering very slightly right, toward the telegraph pole in the **next** field, just behind a hedge. Cross a footbridge just to the left of this pole. Continue to reach the far right corner of the next field.*

A Only earthworks remain now of Bolebec Castle, but they are impressive enough. Your route starts along the line of the outer defences and passes the great, grassy, mound of the motte, where a stone tower once stood. It was probably built in the 11th century. The castle was finally destroyed by Cromwell's soldiers.

B The 13th-century church.

Walk 9
WADDESDON
4 miles (9.6 km) Easy

Estate roads and footpaths combine to encircle Waddesdon Manor, one of the most magnificent feats of architecture in England. The natural beauty of the countryside is enhanced by the fabulous mansion which crowns the tree-clad hill in the centre. The top of Lodge Hill was actually levelled off to provide a flat base for the construction of this building, which rivals the châteaux of the Loire.

Waddesdon Manor

A The cricket pitch on your left occupies the site of the gasworks which supplied Waddesdon Manor between 1883 and 1916. Coal came here by train.

B The short section of hedged track is part of the dismantled tramway which used to run from Quainton to Brill.

C Allow time to visit Waddesdon Manor. Now in the care of the National Trust, it is open Easter – Oct. Wed – Sun (NB. open on Bank Hol. Mons but closed the following Wed). The house will be closed in 1990 for major works, but the grounds, aviary, shops and restaurant will remain open. The house will re-open in 1991. The estate was purchased from the Duke of Marlborough by Baron Ferdinand de Rothschild in 1874. The Baron set about having a French château built, with mature trees replanted around it. The Prince of Wales came to the housewarming party in 1883. Queen Victoria herself came to see the house in 1890. The village was to benefit in other ways from Baron Ferdinand de Rothschild's decision to settle in Waddesdon. The village almshouses were modernised, the Five Arrows Hotel was built (the Rothschild crest has five arrows) and a village hall was built.

Over

20

0   1 mile

0   1 km

5 Enter a short section of hedged track, but turn right immediately over a stile. Go diagonally across this field, to the left. Cross a stile where the second line of electricity pylons crosses the hedge. Continue across the next field to a gateway.

6 Bear slightly right after going through the gateway. Walk with a fence on your right to a fenced farm track. Proceed along this track back to Waddesdon, passing a nursery garden on your left. Turn right along the A41 back to the War Memorial.

1 Start from the War Memorial in Waddesdon. This is on the A41 at the western end of the village, which is 6 miles (9.6 km) west of Aylesbury, from where there is a frequent weekday bus service. Cars can be parked nearby.
Go down the estate road (signed 'Windmill Hill Farm') away from the A41. Tall gate-posts mark your entry to the park of Waddesdon Manor. Cross an estate road, pass a bowling green on your right and go ahead across another estate road.

Westcott

Waddesdon

A41

Lodge Hill

Waddesdon Manor

Westcott Field Farm

Windmill Hill Farm

2 Bend right with the road, then left to descend to Windmill Hill Farm. Keep the farmhouse well on your left as you follow the track through the farmyard, turning left and almost immediately right, then left and right again to a gate. Go down the concrete farm track.

3 Pass houses on your left, continue through a gate ahead and descend with a fence on your right. Go through a gate ahead and turn right to walk with a hedge on your right. Go through a gate ahead and cross a field to another gate. You cross another path to walk with a hedge on your right to another gate. Go ahead with a fence on your left and a hedge on your right to reach Westcott Field Farm.

4 Go ahead to the road and turn right towards the village of Westcott. Look for a turning on your left to the Royal Ordnance Factory. Almost immediately after this, turn right over a stile. Go ahead to where the first line of electricity pylons crosses the hedge ahead, at a gateway.

Walk 10
NOTLEY ABBEY
6 miles (9.6 km) Easy

The ruins of the old Augustinian abbey at Notley are not open to the public, so it is fortunate that a public footpath runs beside the old walls, giving a good view of what remains. The villages of Haddenham and Chearsley have mud walling, called witchert (chopped straw mixed with clay), and the field paths afford fine views. This used to be a major area for duck-rearing.

5 *Ignoring a stile on your right, go downhill with a hedge on your right. Cross a stile and turn left along a track for 90 yards (81 m). Cross a stile ahead and continue to two gates in the far corner. Take the gate on the right and cross the field diagonally.*

4 *Go ahead with a fence on your right, descending to a stile and on to a woodland path. Cross a stile to a field ahead. Continue with a fence on your right to cross a stile ahead. Go uphill in the next field, veering very slightly right to the top of the hill.*

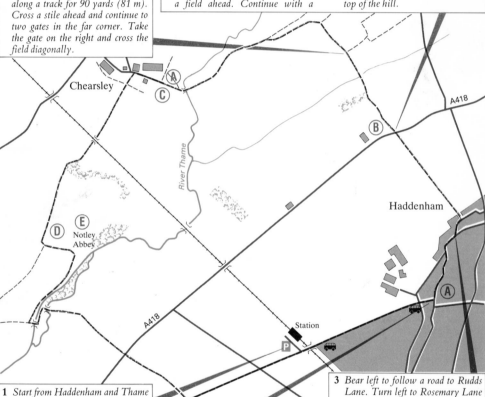

Chearsley

River Thame

A418

Haddenham

Notley Abbey

Station

1 *Start from Haddenham and Thame Parkway Station on British Rail's Chiltern Line (Marylebone – Banbury). Cars can be parked here, while buses from Oxford and Aylesbury stop nearby. Turn left to follow the road into Haddenham.*

2 *Turn left just before The Crown, to go up Fern Lane. Go ahead at the end of the lane along a path to the left of the Old Brewery. Emerge at Towns End Green.*

3 *Bear left to follow a road to Rudds Lane. Turn left to Rosemary Lane and go left up the drive of a cottage with distinctive circular brick chimneys called 'Cobweb'. Go ahead over a stile to follow a path with a hedge on your right to the A418. Cross the road carefully and cross the stile ahead.*

Over

0   1 mile

0   1 km

8 *Veer very slightly left to a stile and go left uphill, parallel to an electricity line on your right. Pass Notley Dovecote on your left and reach a farm, where you bear right to cross a stile in the corner of the field near an electricity pylon. Turn left along a track to pass the farmhouse on your left. Cross a stile to the right of a gate to follow a fenced path past Notley Abbey on your left.*

7 *Cross a track to take a stile ahead and continue with a fence on your right. Cross the railway line carefully and go ahead with a fence on your left to a gateway in the corner. Walk with a stream on your left to a footbridge on your left. Cross this footbridge.*

6 *Cross a stile beside a gate ahead. Go ahead with the River Thame on your right to cross a footbridge over it. Head just to the right of the church to take a kissing-gate onto Church Lane. Turn left opposite Shupps Lane to follow a path to a stile in a fence ahead.*

Chearsley

A418

9 *Turn right over a stile across a field to another stile. Continue to a gate on your left, leading to a bridge over the old millraces.*

10 *Follow a path on your left, then cross a footbridge on the right. Go ahead to cross a stile and go on until you reach the A418. Cross it carefully and continue along the signposted path ahead. When you reach a road, turn left along it back to the start.*

Haddenham

Notley Abbey

A418

Station

A The walls bordering these lanes provide good examples of witchert.

B This is Roundhill and a tumulus can still be discerned on your left.

C Some grassy mounds reveal that Chearsley used to stand between the church and the River Thame, until the village was moved following the Black Death

in 1348.

D Notley Abbey's old dovecote.

E The remains of Notley Abbey.

WING

4 miles (6.4 km) Easy, but can be muddy

0   1 mile

0   1 km

Wing, which is derived from the Anglo-Saxon 'Weowum's People', stands on a ridge overlooking the Vale of Aylesbury. The gentle, rolling contours and the lightly wooded character of this area give a feeling of lightness and space, and there is a sense of remoteness. These paths can be very muddy after wet weather, especially where cattle have congregated at gateways, so come prepared!

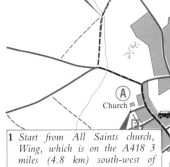

2 *Cross the stream on your right at a footbridge. Veer left to cross a stile beside a gate in the top corner of the field. Go along a lane to a road at a telephone box. Go ahead through a signposted gap in the hedge and follow a concrete farm road until it bears left.*

3 *Turn right over a stile and turn left immediately to go on.*

Burcott Hall Farm

Long Spinney

Burcott

Waterloo Farm

Church

(A)   Wing   Ascott House (B)

Lower Ascott

4 *Cross a stile and a footbridge to walk with a hedge on your right up the next field. Continue to a waymarked gate in the top right corner. Go through it and turn left to follow a hedge to the corner of the field occupied by an electricity pylon. Turn sharply right to follow the right of way back across the field to an old gateway in the far hedge. Go ahead across the next field, aiming just to the right of the farm below, towards a gate in the hedge.*

5 *Bear left to the farmyard and leave it by the left of two gates ahead, so that you cross the next field with a hedge on your right. Choose the left one of two gates near each other ahead and bear left to cross this field to a stile leading to an estate road. Turn left to reach the A418.*

1 *Start from All Saints church, Wing, which is on the A418 3 miles (4.8 km) south-west of Leighton Buzzard. Cars can be parked near the church. Wing is served by bus nos 65, X13, X14 and X15, on the route between Aylesbury and Milton Keynes. From the church gate, go down Church Street to the High Street and turn left, passing the Cock Inn on your right. At the road junction at the end of the village, turn left toward Winslow. Cross a bridge over a stream and go ahead 30 yards (27 m), then turn right*

7 *Turn sharp right to head for a gap in an earth bank and veer left after it to reach a stile in a fence. Continue to a gate in the top corner of the field and turn right, along a road into Wing. If you came by bus, the bus stop is ahead at The Dove, while Church Street is ahead on your left.*

6 *Turn right along the pavement until you see a signposted footpath on your left. Cross the road carefully to pass allotments on your right. Bear left over a stile and fork right to walk beside a hedge on your right. Go on through woodland to a fenced, waymarked path to a stile giving access to a field. Go ahead to a gate which leads to a concrete farm road, but don't go through it!*

through a gateway and cross a field with the stream on your right.

A Sir John Betjeman called All Saints church, Wing, 'the most important Saxon church in the country'. It dates from the 10th century and may have been built by Elgiva, the widow of the Saxon king, Edwy, who died in 959. One vicar, Dr Dodd, was hung at Tyburn in 1777 for forgery.

B Ascott House (National Trust) is open to the public.

GREAT HAMPDEN

0 _____ 1 mile
0 _____ 1 km

3 miles (4.8 km) Easy, but can be muddy

This is a leafy, if muddy, walk in the home village of Oliver Cromwell's cousin John Hampden, who refused to pay the illegally levied Ship Money to Charles I in 1635. Known as 'the Patriot' for his loyalty to his countrymen, Hampden became an early casualty of the Civil War. He was mortally wounded at the battle of Chalgrove Field in 1643 and lies buried in St Mary Magdalene's church.

5 *Turn right along a waymarked path. At the corner of a field, cross a track on your left and turn right as waymarked, beside Grim's Ditch. Near the end of a line of trees on your left, go right to continue with the fence on your left towards Hampden House.*

4 *The trees change from broadleaved to evergreen. Keep alongside Grim's Ditch until a track leads to the edge of the trees on your right. Turn left as waymarked along the edge of the wood, with a view of Hampden House away to your right. Go on to a track junction.*

6 *When the track bends right, go ahead through a gate and continue to a white gate. Pass Hampden House to your left and the church to your right. Turn right through the churchyard and leave it by a kissing-gate in its back fence. Go ahead with a fence on your right to negotiate another kissing-gate. Pass a pond on your left to pass through a third kissing-gate.*

Ⓐ

Barne's Grove

Ⓑ Hampden House

St Mary Magdalene's Church

Grim's Ditch

Redland End

Great Hampden

7 *Go ahead through another gate to pass a mound on your left. Go straight on across a track and a field. Walk with trees on your right to reach a lane. Go left, back to the start.*

Hampden Row

Keepershill Wood

Ⓟ

3 *Fork right at the road junction to take a signposted footpath on your left, as you face up this road. Go ahead along the path to a stile and cross it to turn right along a lane. Bear left for 20 yards (18 m) at the next road junction and turn right along a signposted footpath into the trees. Walk alongside the linear earthwork, Grim's Ditch.*

2 *Fork right along a waymarked path. Cross a stile at the corner of a road and go ahead. Ignore a path signposted on your left.*

1 *Start from The Hampden Arms in Hampden Row (car parking close by). This is about 6 miles (9.6 km) north of High Wycombe, from where there is a bus service (Beeline 333/334). Go left along the road signposted to Speen, but bear right, away from Speen, at a fork. Follow this lane to a footpath signpost on the left. Turn left into the trees.*

A Grim's Ditch is an ancient linear earthwork. It probably dates from the Iron Age and marked an agreed, peaceful, boundary.

B Hampden House is not open to the public. Hampden's grave is inside St Mary Magdalene's church nearby. His tomb was opened in 1828 and it was proved that Hampden died when his own pistol burst because his servant had loaded it without removing any former charges.

GREAT MISSENDEN

3.8 miles (6.1 km) Moderate, can be muddy in places

0   1 mile
0   1 km

The stations along British Rail's line through the Chilterns from Marylebone to Aylesbury give easy access to some wonderful walking country. The paths are in superb condition, being well used and waymarked. The only problem is mud in wet weather. The glory of this walk is when the path plunges into woods which seem to deny the presence of houses nearby. In May you can enjoy the bluebells.

5 Turn right up the concrete road to Prestwood Farm. Follow the sign to a stile ahead. Go over a second stile and then a third, ignoring tracks on either side. Go ahead with the hedge on your right. Your path converges with a track on your right, then forks right into woods. Continue through the trees, ignoring paths going to the right.

6 Leave the woods by the narrow path ahead, with a fence on your right and a hedge on your left. Go down to a road and turn right along it. Turn left up a signposted path and veer left as waymarked 'GM70'. Go right, through trees to the ridge. Turn right to walk beside the hedge on your right down to a gap in the bottom corner.

7 Follow the path across the next field to a waymarked stile ahead on the right and go on to a tunnel under the railway on your left. Turn right after going through the tunnel and cross a stile in the corner of the field to then go right along a road. Turn right, as signposted, to the station.

1 Start from Great Missenden station on British Rail's Marylebone to Aylesbury line. Cars may be parked here.
Turn left out of the station yard and left again to cross the road bridge over the railway. Turn left down a private road which is also a public path. Continue past Bernards Close on your right.

2 Turn right up a track, passing a cemetery on your left. Go ahead to woods. Ignore a signposted path on your right in the woods but go ahead through a kissing-gate to walk with a hedge on your right.

3 Go ahead across a field to pick up the hedge on your right again and continue along a narrow path between houses to a road. Go ahead along New Road opposite.

Rignall Wood

Great Missenden

A413

Prestwood

A4128

Angling Spring Wood

Station

P

Ⓐ

4 Cross another road and continue along the narrow, hedged, footpath facing you. Turn right at another road (Nairdwood Lane). Cross the road ahead to go up Moat Lane.

A Great Missenden used to have an abbey. It was built out of gratitude for rescue from shipwreck by William de Missenden in 1133. The abbey's position on a main route to London soon led to it becoming large and wealthy as the rich tried to secure a place in heaven with donations to the abbey. The monks, known as the Black Canons, soon wielded great influence locally, but spiritual corruption followed, with an Abbot dismissed after a visitation in 1236. Another Abbott had a scandalous relationship with a woman in 1530. Henry VIII's Dissolution seemed to be deserved.

HUGHENDEN MANOR

3 miles (4.8 km) Moderate

0 — — — — — 1 mile
0 — — — — 1 km

These 3 miles (4.8 km) seem to encapsulate the essence of Buckinghamshire. A manor house that belonged to a famous politician is set in some magnificent countryside. Beech trees shelter bluebells in May, when the woods are possibly even more attractive than in the autumn. Only the well-trodden paths seem to indicate the proximity of a town, from which buses provide access.

6 *Go ahead along a track. After the last house on your left, cross a stile ahead and bear right through the wood, with its edge never far away on your right. Reach a lane at a signpost and go right.*

7 *Turn right over a stile to follow a signposted path. Keep beside the hedge on your right after crossing a stile in the corner ahead. When you reach woodland on your right, watch for a stile in the fence on your right. Cross it to bear left along a woodland path. Bear right when you see a forest track and keep to this route all the way back to Hughenden Manor. Then retrace your steps back to the start.*

1 *Take the A4128 north of High Wycombe. After 2 miles (3.2 km), a signpost points to Hughenden Manor on your left. If coming by public transport, the bus stop is right next to the sign (there are frequent Beeline buses nos 323/ 324 from High Wycombe and Aylesbury). Go up the signposted lane to the church of St Michael and All Angels, before which is a place for parking cars. Cars can also be parked further on, as signposted, by visitors to Hughenden Manor.*
Start by walking through the churchyard, passing the church on your right.

2 *Go ahead along the uphill path to a small gate, which gives access to the lane. Bear left along it to pass Hughenden Manor on your left.*

5 *Fork right to follow a bank of earth on your right. Cross a stile ahead and walk between a house on your left and a field on your right to a kissing-gate.*

4 *Go ahead to enter more woods. Keep to the main path ahead, ignoring side paths. Pass a small gate on your right and turn right along a clear track just beyond it.*

3 *Go down a signposted bridleway through the trees. Ignore paths on both sides and emerge from the woodland along a fenced path.*

A St Michael and All Angels church, Hughenden, is where Disraeli chose to be buried. He was, perhaps, the greatest of all the politicians to come out of Buckinghamshire. Queen Victoria, who regarded 'Dizzy' with such great affection, came here soon after his burial in 1881 and laid a wreath of her former prime minister's favourite primroses on his tomb. Disraeli's admirers then started the practice of wearing primroses in their buttonholes on the first anniversary of his death on 19th April, thus starting the Prim-rose League.

B Hughenden Manor, which Disraeli bought in 1847, is now in the care of the National Trust. It is open Apr – Oct. Wed – Sat. 2 – 6; Sun and Bank Hol. Mon 12 – 6; and Sat & Sun 2 – 6 in Mar (closed on Good Fri). The withered primroses that Queen Victoria brought are preserved in Dizzy's room.

MILTON'S COTTAGE

5.5 miles (8.8 km) Easy

This walk is across some of the most revered ground in England. A 'pretty box' of a cottage which served the great poet John Milton as a home for less than one year at Chalfont St Giles is connected by footpaths to the Friends Meeting House at Jordans. In the latter's graveyard lie the bones of Thomas Ellwood, the Quaker who found the cottage for Milton as a refuge from the plague in London. Despite the proximity of roads and houses, this is a walk of peace and tranquility, as befits the place where Milton found Paradise.

A Arrange to come here when you can visit the quaint little cottage with the well-tended garden that was Milton's home from May 1665 to April 1666. It is open Mar – Oct. Tue – Sat. & Bank Hols. 10 – 1 and 2 – 6 (or dusk, if earlier). The only one of Milton's homes still standing, it was bought by public subscription in 1887 in honour of Queen Victoria's Jubilee (with the Queen herself donating £20). Milton fled here from London to avoid the plague. He was Cromwell's Latin Secretary, was now blind and living under King Charles II. His epic poem *Paradise Lost* was dictated to his daughter Deborah. Milton's former pupil, Thomas Ellwood, had been honoured to find this refuge for Milton, but wasn't able to welcome the poet because of an unfortunate incident which illustrates the times in which they lived. Ellwood, with his friend Isaac Pennington, were arrested while at the funeral of Edward Perot, a Quaker who tried to convert the pope in order to solve the religious difficulties caused by Charles 11's 'Clarendon Code' (meant to put down Presbyterianism in England). When Ellwood was released one month later, he went to see Milton and was given a manuscript to read and comment upon. It was *Paradise Lost*. Tom said, 'Thou hast said much here of paradise lost, but what hast thou to say of Paradise found?'. Later, when Ellwood was visiting Milton in London, Milton gave him another manuscript to read. It was *Paradise Regained*.

B Jordans is owned by the Quakers (the Society of Friends) and the guest house and conference centre which you pass on this walk is now a place of pilgrimage. Quakers used to meet here in secret before the Toleration Act of 1688. It is the great barn that holds most interest. Not only would it have been where the early Friends met, but it is undoubtedly built with timbers taken from the 'Mayflower', the ship which took the Pilgrim Fathers to America, and is now called the Mayflower Barn. Salt has impregnated the wood, and one of the beams which must have come from the ship's stern has the letters R HAR I. This is all that remains of MAYFLOWER HARWICH. The barn is still used in the summer for concerts and many other events.

C The Meeting House is a simple structure, built in 1688 when the Toleration Act permitted its erection. Isaac Pennington's widow Lady Springett provided the money, and outside in the grounds are the graves of many leading Quakers, including Thomas Ellwood (1639-1713) and William Penn, his wives Gulielma and Hannah and 10 of his 16 children. Gulielma was the daughter of Lady Springett. Penn was arrested for preaching and charged that 'with force of arms he did assemble to the disturbance of the peace'. The jury found Penn guilty only of preaching, so the Lord Mayor of London, who sat on the Bench, refused to dismiss them until they found the verdict he desired. In one of the greatest moments of English history, the jury still found Penn not guilty and were themselves fined and imprisoned, thus highlighting the suppression of freedom of speech. This imprisonment of the jury was appealed against and found to be unlawful. Penn went on to form a State in America to be based on Quaker principles - Pennsylvania.

Over

0   1 mile
0   1 km

8 Go ahead through the kissing-gate and continue to the corner of the next field. Do not go over the stile ahead, however. Turn right over another stile and go ahead to a field. Veer left with a hedge to the left-hand corner. Go left along the hedged path to a road. Cross the road to a pavement and turn left along it.

7 Turn right to follow the public footpath to a gate. Go ahead along this well-defined path, passing Austen's farmhouse on your left. Cross a stile in the hedge ahead to reach your outward path and go ahead with the hedge now on your right.

2 Go down this signposted path, which is well-defined. Pass a greyhound training track on your left, continue past woodland and turn right along a path to a stile in the left hand corner ahead. Walk with the hedge on your left. Go through a kissing-gate to the corner of the next field.

1 Start from Milton's Cottage, Chalfont St Giles, on the B4442. There is a bus stop at Milton's Cottage (London Transport no 305) but motorists will have to park in a side road (Hillside Close is nearest) and walk back to the cottage, which is opposite Milton's Restaurant.

With your back to Milton's Cottage (and facing Milton's Restaurant), turn left to walk up to a roundabout. Go ahead to a public footpath signposted on your left.

Chalfont St Giles

B4442

Ⓐ Milton's Cottage

Dibden Hill

Austens

Jordans

Grove Farm

Ⓑ
Ⓒ

9 Turn right along a signposted path and fork left. Turn right and go ahead to a signposted footpath on your left. Follow this to the road, passing sports fields on your left, and go right to Milton's Cottage.

3 Don't go over the stile ahead, but do turn left over another stile and walk with a hedge on your right, crossing three stiles, and veer left to the far corner. Cross a farm access lane, using stiles in the fences on each side of it, but don't go ahead across the stile in the far corner.

4 Turn sharply right to follow the path with the wood on your left back to a stile giving access to the farm access lane. Go across to a stile beside a gate and walk with a hedge on your right. Cross a stile and go ahead over a second stile to reach the road at Jordans.

5 Turn left to see the Quaker Guest House, the Mayflower Barn and the Friend's Meeting House, all on your left.

6 Retrace your steps up the road. Go past the first signpost (indicating the footpath you have just walked along) and continue to the next public footpath signpost on your right.

BEACONSFIELD

5 miles (8 km) Moderate

The town of Beaconsfield is never far away from this route, demonstrating how easy it is to slip out of the urban environment to enjoy a country walk in Buckinghamshire. Access is made easy by the railway station, which is just around the corner from an impressive and delightful beech wood.

5 Still with the hedge on your right, descend with a narrow path to enter more woodland. Follow a fenced path ahead to a junction where you turn sharply right to follow another fenced path. This leads to Whitchert Close, where you bear left to the B474 road. Go across this road and turn right along the pavement. Turn left along a signposted path opposite the Red Lion. Go ahead, crossing a lane, to reach more woodland. Keep to the waymarked path ahead until the houses end on the right.

4 Go left along the lane, passing a telephone box on your left. Turn right up the track before the road junction, however. Go ahead to a stile by Lilac Cottage. Cross this and go over a second stile on your right. Now follow a long path, keeping a hedge on your right and bending left to go ahead across several stiles.

3 At a grassy clearing on your right, near the railway, veer right through the trees to reach a clear path ahead close to the edge of the wood. Turn right along this and bend right with it, climbing to reach a stile ahead. Cross this but ignore other stiles at this path junction by turning left downhill and across a field to a stile in the far corner.

6 Turn right along a clear woodland path, waymarked with red arrows. This leads to a fenced path, and then to a road. Go ahead to Wilton Road and turn right into Grenfell Road. Turn left at a church, then right down Warwick Road. Turn left to retrace your steps back to the station.

2 Your path joins a track. Bear left along it to reach Woodside Avenue. Go left to Baring Crescent and soon bear right to turn right up Woodside Road. When this road turns right, go ahead along the signposted path to Hogback Wood. Follow the main path on your left.

1 Start at Beaconsfield Station, on British Rail's Chiltern Line from Marylebone to Banbury. Motorists can park their cars at the station. Walk down Station Road and cross it to veer right up Reynolds Road. When this road bends (before the library) go straight ahead along a footpath.

A Children of all ages will be delighted to visit the famous Bekonscot Model Village in Warwick Road. Created in 1929, it is the oldest model village in the world. Open Apr – Oct. 10 – 5 daily, the model's 1.5 acres (0.6 ha) contain a marvellous outdoor model railway, miniature houses, castles, shops, churches and 1200 little people.

The Chilterns are famous for their beech woods and this walk shows you why. Open views add variety, with a magnificent ridge forming the route south of Copy Green. Come in May and the woods would suggest that Bluey's Farm should be renamed Bluebell's.

These Chilterns paths are signposted and waymarked, with stiles in position and a diversion at Bluey's Farm clearly indicated.

3 *Go right, along the lane for 1 mile (1.6 km), then go left of the road sign at Chisbridge Cross to follow the lane to Bluey's Farm. Take the waymarked bridleway on your right, passing the farm on your left.*

4 *Turn right over a stile to walk with a hedge on your left. Cross another stile at the far end of this hedge, go ahead 30 yards (27 m) and bear left over a stile into woodland. Continue along a clear track, ignoring a forest track on your left. Emerge from the forest at the corner of a hedged track on your left.*

5 *Go left up the signposted public bridleway, ignoring the chalky track on your right. Bend right, then left, to climb up to Copy Green. Bear right here along a lane to Copy Farm, where you ignore the signposted bridleway on your left (which is the route of the London Countryway). Instead, go ahead along the footpath through the farmyard, taking the stile to the right of the gate into the field ahead. Walk beside the hedge on your right until it veers right. Veer left to walk beside the hedge on your left downhill to a lane.*

6 *Cross the lane and go up the signposted path opposite, climbing with the hedge on your left. Go over a stile to follow a fenced path to the road, where you turn right, back to the start.*

1 *Park in the quiet lane (with room for vehicles to pass) which forks left towards Marlow Common from the road going north-west from Bovingdon Green, about 1.5 miles (2.4 km) west of Marlow. Walking from the road fork, take the signposted footpath into the wood. The path is waymarked and forks left to reach a signpost. Go ahead across a stile and along a fenced path to the edge of the wood.*

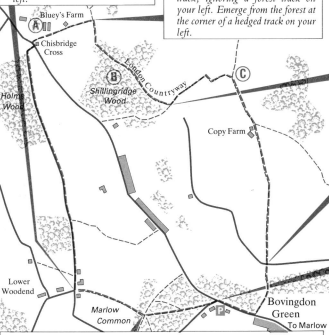

2 *Cross a stile to go downhill to cross a valley track. Go up the other side, as waymarked, with a hedge on your right, to a lane.*

A Bluey's Farm was, until recently, owned by Mr Mavroleon, a Greek ship-owner. It was originally a stud-farm.

B Shillingridge Wood is a fine example of a Chiltern beech wood, although conifers have recently been planted in one corner.

C The London Countryway, a 205 mile walking route around London, shares this circuit from Bluey's Farm to Copy Farm.

0   1 mile

0   1 km

The English Romantic poets were great walkers, so you could well be following in the steps of Percy Bysshe Shelley on this route. Living here both before and after his second marriage, Shelley no doubt knew Happy Valley, which leads from the A4155 up to the broadleaved wood.

5 *Turn right along the road for 50 yards (45 m) to a public footpath signpost on your left. One of its arms points across the road, and you turn right along this track. Fork left off this track to take a waymarked path into woodland and out over a stile. Cross a field to another stile in its far corner and go ahead to a third stile.*

6 *Cross the stile to a path which you bear left along to reach the road at Bovingdon Green. Go right to pass the pond and The Royal Oak on your right, then take a track on your left. Continue along the narrow footpath at the back of Blount's Lodge. This well-defined path between fields forms part of the London Countryway.*

7 *Descend towards Marlow with allotments on your left and houses on your right. Pass a school on your left to reach Queens Road and turn right to reach Oxford Road. Turn left to reach the car park, but don't forget the Marlow Tandoori opposite. As no 47 West Street, this was the home of Thomas Love Peacock.*

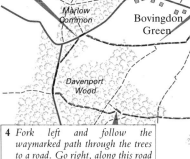

4 *Fork left and follow the waymarked path through the trees to a road. Go right, along this road to a signposted footpath on your right. Follow this to another road.*

3 *Go ahead, ignoring a signposted path on your left. Cross another waymarked stile to follow a hedged path. Cross a third stile ahead to enter woodland. Follow a waymarked path, ignoring the first path that forks left.*

2 *Turn right up the lane signposted as a footpath, soon veering right through a kissing-gate along a narrow path. Walk with a hedge on your left to a stile at the end of the field.*

1 *Start from the car park opposite Marlow Tandoori at the corner of West Street and Oxford Road. West Street is the A4155 to Henley-on-Thames. Marlow has a British Rail station.*
Turn right along the A4155 to walk past Shelley's home and the grammar school. Pass Spinfield Lane and continue to a public footpath signpost on your right.

A Percy Bysshe Shelley (1792-1822) spent two years in Marlow after the tragic suicide of his first wife Harriet in 1816. He brought his mistress, Mary Godwin, to stay at 47 West Street with Thomas Love Peacock, who advised the couple to marry. This they did and leased 104 West Street. Shelley wrote *The Revolt of Islam* here, while Mary wrote *Frankenstein*.

B The Royal Military College was housed in Remnantz from 1802 until its move to Sandhurst in 1812.

C Marlow Grammar School was founded by Sir William Borlase in 1624.

D Thomas Love Peacock lived at 47 West Street, now Marlow Tandoori.

DENHAM

4.5 miles (7.2 km) Easy

0   1 mile

0   1 km

Denham's proximity to film studios led to its charming cottages featuring in several films. The film actor Sir John Mills even lives here. The wonder is that such an attractive place survives and retains its rural character so close to London. If you come by car, park near the church and start the circuit at no **3**. The train is recommended, however.

7 *Cross the stile and turn right to follow a fence on your right down to a stile beside a gate. Go ahead along a hedged bridleway. Pass Moorhouse Farm on your left and bear right. Cross the River Misbourne to reach Higher Denham. Turn right along Lower Road (which becomes Old Rectory Lane). Cross the A412 carefully and go left.*

8 *Turn right through a signposted gap in the hedge and follow a path to join your outward path. Retrace your steps to Denham station but go under the railway along the footpath to reach a road. Turn right for Savay Farm (private). Retrace your steps to the station.*

1 *Start from Denham station, on British Rail's Chiltern Line (Marylebone – Banbury). Park to the north of the station, or by the church. There is a right of way under the station and this walk starts from the southern side (platform one). Follow the path away from the station towards Denham, ignoring a stile on your left and a signposted path on your right.*

2 *Turn left along a signposted path which follows a fence on your right. Cross a cemetery and turn right towards the church.*

3 *Turn right towards the centre of the village. Bear left at the tiny green, cross the bridge over the River Misbourne and bear right to reach the busy A412.*

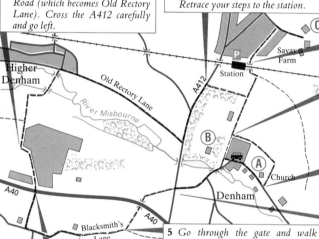

4 *Cross carefully to a signposted stile opposite. Go over the stile and veer slightly left across the field to a stile which leads to a short path. Go ahead to the A40. Go through the gap in the hedge in the central reservation and go ahead on the other side along an old track. Ignore a signposted path on the left and bear right along the track to a gate.*

6 *Cross the A40 and a subsequent estate road carefully. Go ahead along a signposted path between two houses and bear left, as waymarked, to a stile.*

5 *Go through the gate and walk ahead uphill along the lane which enters from the left. Pass Froggy Lane on your left and, opposite Denham Mount, go right along Mount Lane.*

A St Mary's Church, Denham, has a 13th-century font and a brass memorial of Agnes Jordan (died 1554), the last Abbess of Syon at Brentford. Outside are the graves of seven members of the Marshall family, all murdered on Sunday morning, 22nd May, 1870.

B Denham Place was built by Sir Roger Hill between 1688 and 1701. Its grounds were laid out by 'Capability' Brown. In 1729 Sir Roger's son, also called Roger, celebrated his dying father's will with so much alcohol that he died also.

C With parts dating from the 14th century, Savay Farm is the oldest building in Denham. It was once a convalescent home for nuns, who may have bathed in the river. Sir Oswald Mosley lived here before the Second World War and Lady Cynthia Mosley was buried here.

Walk 20
TAPLOW
3.8 miles (6.1 km) Easy

Taplow is probably most familiar as a little station on the main line between Paddington and Reading. Wedged between the urban acres of Slough and the scenic bridge across the River Thames at Maidenhead, Taplow has fine footpaths with good views and lots of historical interest.

2 *Having climbed to a road, turn right to reach the B476 (Berry Hill) and turn left. When you reach the entrance to Taplow Court on your left, turn right to follow a signposted footpath. Walk with trees on your left and a wall or fence on your right, then pass a school playing-field on your left.*

1 *Start from River Road, where there is parking space just south of the A4 on the Buckinghamshire side of Maidenhead bridge. (If you are arriving at Taplow BR station, this is 0.5 mile (0.8 km) east of walk instruction 6 – start the walk here.)*
Walk back to the A4 to cross it (with the bridge on your left) to Mill Lane, opposite. Walk up Mill Lane until a signposted footpath leads right, passing a gas holder on its left. Follow this path.

7 *Cross a stile in the corner of the field and walk with a fence on your right to another stile. Cross this and turn left immediately to walk to the River Thames. Turn right to walk with the river on your left back to the start. Don't forget to try out the echo under Brunel's railway bridge.*

3 *Ignore a waymarked stile on your left and go ahead to reach a road. Turn right to pass Taplow Church on your left. Go ahead along the signposted footpath.*

4 *Go through a kissing-gate and bear right across a field to its far corner, where another kissing-gate gives access to a fenced path. Go left along this. Go through a third kissing-gate and bear right across a field to a road. Turn left to reach the A4.*

5 *Cross the A4 and go ahead to pass a garage on your left. Follow the lane under the railway and past a lake on your left. Ignore a track on your right to Amerden Ponds and go ahead to a public footpath signpost on your right at the junction with the access track from Barge Farm.*

6 *Turn sharply right to follow the waymarked footpath diagonally across a field. Continue along a track across the next field and cross a stream before veering right with this track.*

A Maidenhead Bridge spans the River Thames at a strategic site. There was an ancient ford here and control of it was significant when the Saxons invaded in the fifth century. Ambrosius Aurelianus struggled to hold Taplow's commanding heights for the Britons for 12 years, but the Saxons won them in a bloody battle in about 500. Their leader Tappa (or Aella) gave his name to Taplow and was buried here. Rich finds from his grave are now in the British Museum.

B Taplow Court incorporates the pond where St Birinus baptised the Saxons in the seventh century.

C Taplow Church is a modern building on the Saxon site.

D Brunel's railway bridge, built in 1838, is known as 'the sounding arch' because of its echo.

34

DORNEY AND BOVENEY LOCK
5 miles (8 km) Easy

This is the easiest of walks, both in terms of effort and of finding the way. This level route is shared mostly between the towpath of the River Thames and quiet lanes, and there are plenty of good places to picnic along the way. Dorney was noted in the Domesday Book for its honey and means 'Island of Bees' in Saxon.

3 *When the track forks left, keep going ahead, veering slightly right, with a fence on your right. Go ahead to the River Thames.*

2 *When the road bends right (Marsh Lane), keep going ahead along a signposted footpath which begins as a track.*

1 *Dorney is on the B3026, 2 miles (3.2 km) west of Eton (and on the Beeline bus routes nos 63 and 64). Car parking is usually available on Dorney Common, near the junction with the lane to Boveney. Start the walk by walking through Dorney to reach the gates of Dorney Court on your left. Go on to the next turning on your left and walk down it to pass the church on your left.*

5 *Pass Boveney Lock on your right and turn sharply left along the lane back to Dorney. Turn to see Windsor Castle on your right.*

4 *Turn left to walk with the river on your right.*

Dorney

Church

Dorney Court **A**

B

C

Oakley Court **D**

River Thames

Boveney

Boveney Lock

Chapel **E**

B3026

P

A Dorney Court is a 15th-century manor house which used to belong to the nearby Abbey of Burnham. It is a beautifully preserved example of Tudor timber framing and is open Easter – second Sun in Oct. Sun & Bank Hol. Mons, and Mon & Tue during June, July, Aug & Sept 2 – 5. The first pineapple to be grown in England was produced here for King Charles II.

B The church of St James the Less dates from the 13th century and has a Norman font.

C The Count Dracula horror films were made by Hammer Films in the now rather dilapidated buildings of Bray Studios.

D Oakley Court is in rather better condition, serving as a hotel with attractive riverside grounds.

E It's worth diverting to see the chapel of St Mary Magdalene. This building dates from the 12th century but the site is ancient.

Walk 22
ASHWELL
4.8 miles (7.7 km) Moderate

Broad views into the neighbouring counties of Bedfordshire and Cambridgeshire combine with a strong sense of history in Ashwell to make this an especially interesting walk. The springs that are surrounded by Ash trees are the source of the River Rhee, a tributary of the Cam. The village is an architectural delight. Ashwell was once a town and was recorded in the Domesday Book as one of Hertfordshire's five boroughs. Its weekly market was discontinued in 1792. Today it is a commuter village, even though its station is some distance away.

A The 176 feet (53 m) high tower of St Mary's church, Ashwell, is an elegant landmark for miles around. Inside the church are some rich examples of medieval graffiti. There are several drawings, of which by far the most important is the drawing of old St Paul's. This is to be seen on the inner north wall of the tower together with three other pictures. It is a rare, detailed drawing of an important subject. Drawn with a fine sense of architectural proportion, it shows the old St Paul's cathedral before its spire was destroyed by lightning in 1561. It is possible that we owe this drawing to a mason who had worked on St Paul's prior to working on the church at Ashwell. Also on the inner north wall of the tower is one of the better inscriptions. It can be translated from the Latin to read: '1000, three times 100, five times 10, a pitiable, fierce violent (plague departed); a wretched populace survives to witness (to the plague) and in the end a mighty wind, Maurns, thunders in this year in the world, 1361'. This is one of several inscriptions which refer to the black death which was at its peak in 1349. The 'mighty wind' refers to a great storm in 1361. Ashwell church is also renowned for its choir festival. Each spring, top choirs from around the country come here.

B Ashwell Village Museum began as the private collection of two schoolboys. The local people gave them enthusiastic support, both in adding to the collection and in purchasing this old Tudor house, allowing the museum to open in 1930. It can be visited on Sunday and Bank Holiday Monday afternoons. Nearby are several timber-framed cottages and the Merchant Taylor's School (founded in 1681), which is now a field studies centre. You could divert in an easterly direction along Swan Street. This becomes Hodwell, at the end of which is the old lock-up, built in 1800. From here a path leads to the springs which gave Ashwell its name. Ash trees, holy wells and hod (as in *Hod*well) are all associated with ley, or earth energy, lines according to Alfred Watkins in *The Old Straight Track* (1925).

C An official alternative to the more southerly route of the Icknield Way Path takes this path.

D Arbury Banks is a rampart and ditch enclosing 12.5 acres (5 ha) and surrounding a large circular hut. This may have housed a chieftain. A 'rescue' dig in 1856 found that the V-shaped ditch was 15 feet (4.5 m) deep and 20 feet (6 m) wide. Storage pits and pit dwelling sites were discovered, while numerous examples of the high-shouldered handled jars as found in East Anglia were also found. Bones from deer, goat, horse, pig and long-horned oxen were also found, as was part of a human skull. More skulls had been dug up on an earlier occasion and reburied in Ashwell churchyard.

over

0   1 mile

0   1 km

6 *Veer right with the hedge and descend gradually to Ashwell, whose church spire is a prominent landmark. When you reach a road, turn sharply left along it for a quarter of a mile (400 m). Turn right at a public path signpost and follow an old green lane. Look for a waymark post on your right and turn right as directed by a yellow arrow to follow a footpath. When you reach a stream, don't cross it. Instead, go left to cross a stile in the corner of the hedge and go ahead with the stream on your right.*

1 *Start from the church of St Mary the Virgin, Ashwell. This village is 3 miles (4.8 km) north-west of*

7 *Turn right through a gateway to reach a lane at its corner. Bear right along this lane to Ashwell. Ignore a turning on your left, but fork left at the thatched 'Chain Cottage' to return to Mill Street. The church is on your right.*

the A1 at Letchworth. Ashwell has a station on British Rail's line between London King's Cross and Cambridge via Hitchin. The station is 2 miles (3.2 km) east of the village. Cars can be parked near the church.

Leave by the lych gate and turn left up Mill Street. Cross the road ahead to an old Tudor house which serves as the village museum.

Church

Ashwell

Newnham Hill

Newnham Way

Arbury Banks

2 *Turn right along Swan Street, passing the village cottage garden on your left and the green on your right. Bear left up Gardiners Lane and turn right along the High Street, passing Bear House on your left. Go ahead, passing Wilson's Lane on your left and Farrow's Farm on your right. Continue past Back Street on your left and go up West End to a fork. Look for a signpost on your left, at Partridge Hill. Turn left up this track.*

5 *Turn left along the road for 250 yards (225 m), then turn right up a signposted bridleway, walking with a hedge on your left. Enter a new field and immediately turn right to walk with a hedge on your right and with extensive views over Bedfordshire on your left.*

4 *Leave the enclosed Arbury Banks when another unploughed ridge appears at the corner of the field on your left. Bear left to follow a path at the foot of this. Ignore a downhill path on your right. Pass a hedge going down on your right, then walk beside a plantation of trees on your right. Bear right on a track down to the road.*

3 *Ignore a track on your left and go ahead past a terrace of white cottages on your right. Look for a sign in the hedge on your right. This points to Arbury Banks and is where the right of way leads to it. If you continue ahead for a few yards, you will find a more commonly used clear path on your right. Turn right along this and bear left to walk with the fenced enclosure of Arbury Banks on your right.*

Walk 23

ROYSTON

6 miles (9.7 km) Moderate

Extensive views into Cambridgeshire complement the sense of history provided by ancient chalky tracks past Bronze Age tumuli (round barrows). Therfield Heath is the most extensive barrow cemetery in the Chilterns. Royston's cave has connections with the Knights Templar and, perhaps, the Romans.

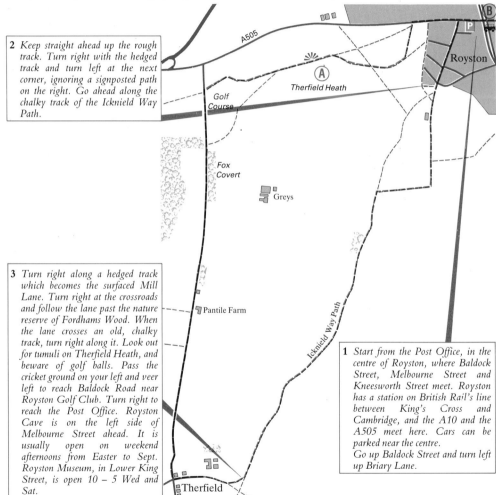

2 *Keep straight ahead up the rough track. Turn right with the hedged track and turn left at the next corner, ignoring a signposted path on the right. Go ahead along the chalky track of the Icknield Way Path.*

3 *Turn right along a hedged track which becomes the surfaced Mill Lane. Turn right at the crossroads and follow the lane past the nature reserve of Fordhams Wood. When the lane crosses an old, chalky track, turn right along it. Look out for tumuli on Therfield Heath, and beware of golf balls. Pass the cricket ground on your left and veer left to reach Baldock Road near Royston Golf Club. Turn right to reach the Post Office. Royston Cave is on the left side of Melbourne Street ahead. It is usually open on weekend afternoons from Easter to Sept. Royston Museum, in Lower King Street, is open 10 – 5 Wed and Sat.*

1 *Start from the Post Office, in the centre of Royston, where Baldock Street, Melbourne Street and Kneesworth Street meet. Royston has a station on British Rail's line between King's Cross and Cambridge, and the A10 and the A505 meet here. Cars can be parked near the centre.*
Go up Baldock Street and turn left up Briary Lane.

A Therfield Heath has tumuli on your right and views on your left. | **B** Royston's cave.

WALLINGTON

4 miles (6.4 km) Easy

0			1 mile
0		1 km	

Wallington has become known as George Orwell's village. Five years after leaving here, *Animal Farm* appeared, set in 'Manor Farm, Willingdon'. Manor Farm, Wallington, is on the route of this walk and near Orwell's cottage. The first half of this walk follows the route of the Icknield Way Path. This passes an early Nonconformist burial ground at Redhill.

6 *Turn left at The Plough to take Kit's Lane, passing George Orwell's cottage (no 2) on your right. Turn left along a signposted path back to the church.*

5 *Reach a hedge and turn left to walk past houses on your right. Go down a track on your right to a lane and turn right.*

4 *Turn left along the road. When you come to a T junction, turn right to follow the road for about 600 yards (550 m). Turn left along a signposted path.*

1 *Start from St Mary's church, Wallington. Cars can be parked considerately nearby (avoid service times). Wallington is about 3 miles (4.8 km) east of Baldock. There is a bus (no. 23) from Royston on Tuesdays and from Buntingford on Saturdays.*
With the church at your back, bear left. When you reach a duck-pond on your left, turn right over a stile and bear right to another stile.

2 *Cross the next field diagonally to its far left corner. Go ahead with a line of trees on your left in the field after that. When the hedge turns left, go ahead to cross a ditch beside a 'Please Keep Dogs on Lead or Under Control' sign. Follow the path which veers left across the next field to reach a lane at a signpost.*

3 *Go left a few paces, then turn right up a signposted track. Go ahead with a hedge on your left, then between two fields before following a hedge on your left again. When this eventually starts to bear right, turn left over a footbridge and a subsequent stile to go across a field to cross another stile just to the left of a house which has solar panels on the roof. Go ahead along the path between two houses to reach a road.*

A George Orwell was the pen-name of Eric Blair. Whilst living in Wallington, he was married in St Mary's church to his first wife, Eileen O'Shaughnessy. The date of the wedding was 9th June, 1936, and photocopies of the marriage certificate can be bought in the church.

B Older residents of Wallington still remember George Orwell as the kind man who kept the village sweet shop. This was the small cottage next to The Plough. He had no previous connection with the area, to which he came for peace and quiet in April 1936. *The Road to Wigan Pier* was written here, but income from the shop was needed to pay the 7s 6d (37½p) weekly rent. He went to Barcelona from here in December 1936 and returned in July 1937. *Homage to Catalonia* was then written here. The couple left this cottage for a flat near Regent's Park in May 1940.

SANDON

0   1 km

5.5 miles (8.9 km) Easy, but expect mud in wet weather

Some parts of this walk can be very muddy in wet weather, so come here after a dry spell if you can. It would be a shame to miss these old green lanes as they provide the route with such character, as well as shade on a hot, sunny day. The conditions underfoot don't just depend on the weather. These paths are popular with riders and their horses' hooves damage the surface.

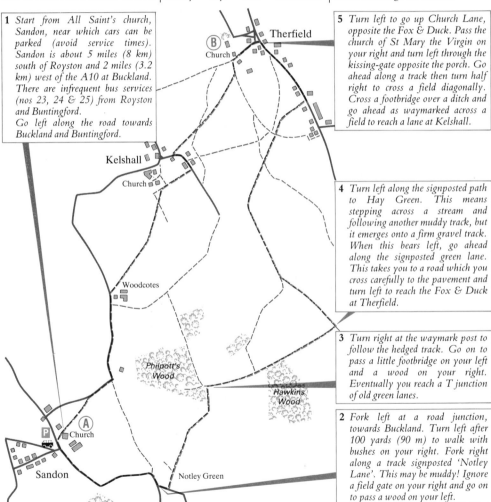

1 *Start from All Saint's church, Sandon, near which cars can be parked (avoid service times). Sandon is about 5 miles (8 km) south of Royston and 2 miles (3.2 km) west of the A10 at Buckland. There are infrequent bus services (nos 23, 24 & 25) from Royston and Buntingford.*
Go left along the road towards Buckland and Buntingford.

5 *Turn left to go up Church Lane, opposite the Fox & Duck. Pass the church of St Mary the Virgin on your right and turn left through the kissing-gate opposite the porch. Go ahead along a track then turn half right to cross a field diagonally. Cross a footbridge over a ditch and go ahead as waymarked across a field to reach a lane at Kelshall.*

4 *Turn left along the signposted path to Hay Green. This means stepping across a stream and following another muddy track, but it emerges onto a firm gravel track. When this bears left, go ahead along the signposted green lane. This takes you to a road which you cross carefully to the pavement and turn left to reach the Fox & Duck at Therfield.*

3 *Turn right at the waymark post to follow the hedged track. Go on to pass a little footbridge on your left and a wood on your right. Eventually you reach a T junction of old green lanes.*

2 *Fork left at a road junction, towards Buckland. Turn left after 100 yards (90 m) to walk with bushes on your right. Fork right along a track signposted 'Notley Lane'. This may be muddy! Ignore a field gate on your right and go on to pass a wood on your left.*

Over

40

7 *When the hedge ends on your right, maintain your direction across an open field to reach a footpath signpost near the corner of a lane. Turn left along this lane and follow it as it bears right. Turn left over a stile beside a signpost and cut across a corner to a stile in the next fence. Continue in this direction to a third stile in another fence, near a pond on your left.*

8 *Maintain your direction by going ahead along the right of way which crosses the next field diagonally. Pass within 50 yards (45 m) of the corner of the hedge on your right and continue to gradually converge with the hedge ahead on your left at a clump of trees, where the hedge forms a small corner. Look for an old, broken stile here and cross it to continue in the same direction. Aim just to the right of farm buildings ahead and go ahead across a track in the middle of this field. Finally reach the corner formed by hedgerows and emerge on a lane at a signpost.*

9 *Turn left along the lane, which bends right. Fork left for 300 yards (270 m) after this bend at the 'Sandon' sign and walk up a narrow hedged path. This emerges at the churchyard. Carry on, passing the church on your left to reach the church gate by the road.*

6 *Turn left along the lane. Pass a house on the left called 'The Maltings', then a bungalow on your right. Just after this, turn right along a signposted path.*

B Therfield
Church

Kelshall
Church

Woodcotes

Philpott's Wood

Hawkins Wood

A
P
Church

Sandon

Notley Green

A All Saints' Church, Sandon, is of Saxon origin and was granted by King Athelstan to the Dean and Chapter of St Paul's. It remained in their possession for nearly one thousand years, until the mid 19th century. Of special interest are the brass memorials before the Chancel steps. These are to the 15th-century Lord and Lady of Danyells. Two of their daughters were called Elizabeth.

B St Mary's Church, Therfield, contains memorials to the Turner family. The Rev. Francis Turner was one of the 'Seven Bishops' sent to the Tower in 1688 for petitioning James II against his Declaration of Indulgence.

PIRTON

4 miles (6.4 km) Easy

0   1 mile

0   1 km

This walk is close to Hitchin, but it was also a part of the country familiar to the Ancient Britons, who trod these chalk tracks. The village of Pirton is well-supplied with pubs and has a church with an interesting history. Opposite the church is Toot Hill. Mounds named after Tout (the Celtic god of pathways) were recognised by Alfred Watkins in his book *The Old Straight Track* (1925) as mark-points on trackways.

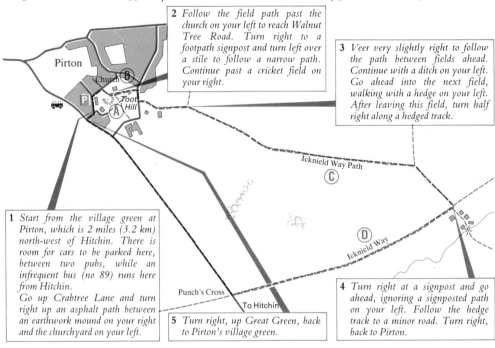

2 *Follow the field path past the church on your left to reach Walnut Tree Road. Turn right to a footpath signpost and turn left over a stile to follow a narrow path. Continue past a cricket field on your right.*

3 *Veer very slightly right to follow the path between fields ahead. Continue with a ditch on your left. Go ahead into the next field, walking with a hedge on your left. After leaving this field, turn half right along a hedged track.*

Pirton

Church B

P

Toot Hill A

H

Icknield Way Path C

Icknield Way D

1 *Start from the village green at Pirton, which is 2 miles (3.2 km) north-west of Hitchin. There is room for cars to be parked here, between two pubs, while an infrequent bus (no 89) runs here from Hitchin.*
Go up Crabtree Lane and turn right up an asphalt path between an earthwork mound on your right and the churchyard on your left.

Punch's Cross

To Hitchin

5 *Turn right, up Great Green, back to Pirton's village green.*

4 *Turn right at a signpost and go ahead, ignoring a signposted path on your left. Follow the hedge track to a minor road. Turn right, back to Pirton.*

A A Norman motte and bailey castle once stood here, built on an ancient site – Toot Hill.

B St Mary's church, Pirton, was built as a cruciform church about 1100. The tower as built was unstable,and centuries of neglect led to the Rev. Ralph Loughborough mounting a massive appeal for the church's restoration in 1875. The vicar and his wife were sent thousands of shillings from all over Britain. Villagers gave their labour voluntarily and even built a new south transept in 1913 as a memorial to the vicar and his wife who had served Pirton so well for nearly half a century.

C This is the route of the modern Icknield Way Path. This long distance path runs for 104 miles (167 km) from the Ridgeway Path at Ivinghoe Beacon to the Peddars Way Path at Knettishall Heath.

D This is the route of the ancient Icknield Way. Its name was derived from the late Iron Age Iceni tribe. The Way runs over the chalk, avoiding the clay that often caps the ridges. The soils are light in texture and this is open country.

TELEGRAPH HILL

3.8 miles (6.1 km) Moderate

This, one of the best-preserved sections of the Icknield Way could tempt even the most fainthearted into setting off on a long distance walk. The way is clear to Dorset. This short walk along part of the Way offers excellent views over Bedfordshire. John Bunyan may have had Telegraph Hill in mind when he wrote about 'delectable mountains'. Beech and birch trees clothe its slopes.

2 *Pass a clump of trees on your left. This is Telegraph Hill and you pass its nature reserve on your right. Go downhill to a path junction and turn left. Climb with the path to pass a tumulus on your right. Bear left here across a field.*

1 *Take the B655 road west from Hitchin. After 3 miles (4.8 km) there is a Bedfordshire road sign, on your left. This is near the entrance to a signposted bridleway and there is space to park a car considerably.*
Go up the signposted bridleway. This hedged track is part of the Icknield Way. The county boundary runs down its centre, so keep to the left if you wish to stay in Hertfordshire! You soon pass a stile on your right, but climb gradually for 1 mile (1.6 km) to pass a waymark post on your right. Ignore a signposted bridleway on your left. Go ahead with the hedge on your right.

5 *Pass a patch of woodland on your right and go ahead across the corner of the field. Bear left along an access lane to pass Wellbury House on your right. Go ahead along a rough track on the right hand edge of a field. Bear left to pass a path junction on your right. Pass a cottage called 'Woodland' on your right and go ahead along a track to the B655 road. Turn left to walk back carefully to the Bedfordshire road sign.*

4 *The path curves left through the wood to emerge at the corner of a field. Go ahead with a hedge on your right. Pass the Tudor house at Little Offley on your right and go ahead along a signposted bridleway. When the farm track bends right, keep straight on down a field path.*

3 *Go past a signpost to walk with a hedge on your right to another signpost. Turn left here across a field to a corner of a wood. Walk past trees on your right for 20 yards (18 m), then bear right along a path into the wood.*

A The Icknield Way is an ancient route along the chalk 'spine' of southern England. It linked with the Ridgeway at Goring to provide a through route from Norfolk to Dorset and ran parallel with the higher Ridgeway into Wiltshire.

B Telegraph Hill was the site of a semaphore signalling station used by The Admiralty to transmit the news of Trafalgar and Waterloo. A racecourse once existed here and the deep ruts were made by the carriages of the racegoers.

C This tumulus (a burial mound or sighting mound) is one of the many near the Icknield Way.

D Little Offley has a fine Tudor house. King Offa is said to have died nearby.

KNEBWORTH PARK

4.3 miles (6.9 km) Easy

A pleasant walk through a country park complete with deer leads to a house full of interest and history. Knebworth has been the home of the Lytton family for centuries. The first Viceroy of India, Robert, first Earl of Lytton, lived here, as did his son Victor (Acting Viceroy and Governor of Bengal). The grounds have been given over to pop concerts in recent years.

A This obelisk was built by Sir Edward Bulwer Lytton as a memorial to his mother. He didn't erect it until 1866, however, some 23 years after her death. Against his domineering mother's wishes, he had married a beautiful but hysterical Irish girl, Rosina Wheeler. His mother had stopped his allowance in consequence and his dead father's bequest of £200 failed to meet his wife's extravagances. Bulwer was penniless at the start of a career as a writer and his wife turned savagely against her overworked husband, whom she perceived as neglecting her. The marriage failed, but Bulwer went on alone to become a successful novelist.

B Look for a Bronze Age tumulus to the right of the path as it enters Graffridge Wood.

C The original Knebworth was a small manor house belonging to a knight called Eudo Dapifer, a steward to William the Conqueror. It is recorded in the Domesday Book as Chenepeworde, meaning the house on the hill. The Lytton family came here in 1492 and it remained an essentially Tudor building until Elizabeth Bulwer Lytton started a radical renovation programme. This ended when Sir Edward Bulwer Lytton, who came back to Knebworth when his mother died in 1843, modernised the house in Victorian Gothic style. The towers were capped with copper domes and the house was embellished with gargoyles and battlements. The east front retains a Tudor appearance and the banqueting hall where Elizabeth I was entertained in 1588 has a minstrels' gallery dating from 1610, and a Jacobean oak screen. Bulwer wrote how the spirit of romance in his novels 'was greatly due to their having been written at my ancestral home, Knebworth. How could I help writing romances', he said, 'after living among the secret panels and hiding-places of our dear ancestors as I peered into the shadowy abysses of the secret chamber. It was years before I could venture inside without my hair literally bristling with terror'. Bulwer anticipated Dickens by writing about the terrible prison conditions and harsh penal code of the time in his first novels, *Paul Clifford, Eugene Aram, Pelham* and *The Disowned*. Mysticism crept into his splendid *Last Days of Pompeii*. A man of many parts, Bulwer also became an M.P., first for St Ives, then for Lincoln.

As a Liberal, he campaigned for the victims of 'low birth and iron fortune'. Friendship with Disraeli led him to cross the floor of the House and, as Colonial Secretary, to deliver a speech which Palmerston described to Queen Victoria as the best he had ever heard in the House of Commons. He was also a dramatist and, together with his friend Dickens, founded the Guild of Literature and Art. They gave performances in the banqueting hall to raise money to subsidise poor 'men of letters'. Bulwer's most haunting work is his novel *The Coming Race*, in which he prophesied the destructive force of nuclear weapons. Knebworth House is open late May – mid Sept. 12 – 5 daily. Among its attractions is a collection of railway memorabilia, a model railway layout and a narrow gauge railway in the park.

D The mausoleum was built in the Grecian style in 1817 to contain the remains of Elizabeth Bulwer Lytton. A quarrelsome character, she fell out with the local rector and wouldn't set foot in the church. The cremated remains of Lady Constance Lytton, a leader of the Suffragettes, were also set here when she died in 1923.

E The church of the Virgin Mary and St Thomas of Canterbury serves the village as well as the house.

Over

4 *The path aims for a gap in the hedge ahead. Continue alongside the right hand edge of the next field, then past a wood on your right. Go ahead over a stile beside a gate and cut across the next field to wooden bars in the fence to the right of the opposite corner. Go ahead through scrub, then bear right.*

5 *Cross a stile beside a gate in the corner and climb up to the B656 road. Cross it and take the signposted path ahead, with woodland on your left. Turn right at a waymark post to follow a path across the field to a stile beside a gate. Pass a small wood on your right and go ahead to a farm.*

6 *Go ahead through the farmyard, as signposted, and cross a field to a stile beside a gate. Go straight on across the next field to take a path into the woodland of Knebworth Park. Veer right at a 'private' sign to follow the public path to a ladder stile in the fence. Go left, with the fence on your left to a tree-lined concrete track on your right. Take this to Knebworth House and bear left to the church. Leave this by the lych gate to go ahead past the cricket pavilion on your left. Turn right along the road back to the Lytton Arms.*

Burleigh Farm

Gaffridge Wood

Wintergreen Wood

Mausoleum

B656

B

Knebworth Country Park

D

E

Church

C

Knebworth House

3 *Cross this road (the B656) and take the signposted path ahead over a footbridge and into Graffridge Wood. The path keeps to the edge of the wood at first, then bears left into the trees. Notice the tumulus on your right. Go ahead, ignoring crosspaths, to a lane. Turn right to pass 'Keepers Cottage' on your left. Just after a second cottage on your left, turn right along a signposted footpath.*

A

P

Old Knebworth   To Knebworth (Station)

2 *Go ahead with a hedge on your right. At the far corner, bear right through woodland and turn left after crossing a stile to go over a ladder stile into a deer park. Pass a monument on your right and keep the hedge on your left. Veer right with the trees that are met on your left to cross a ladder stile in the fence ahead. Continue with a fence on your left to go over another ladder stile ahead and reach a road.*

1 *Start from the Lytton Arms, Old Knebworth. This is 1 mile (1.6 km) west of Knebworth and 2 miles south of Stevenage, where there are railway stations. An infrequent bus (no 44) connects Old Knebworth with Stevenage and Luton. Cars can be parked carefully near the Lytton Arms.*
With your back to this inn, cross the road to the pavement and turn left, passing almshouses on your left. Pass Park Gate House on your right and turn right to cross a stile beside a gate.

SHAW'S CORNER
5.5 miles (8.8 km) Easy

This corner of Hertfordshire contains several towns, with the urban sprawl of Luton contained just across the Bedfordshire border. Here is a haven of rural peace, however, as desired by George Bernard Shaw, the great dramatist who made his home here in the first half of the 20th century. There are gentle hillsides, woods, a stream with watercress beds and an unusual church.

A This church was built in 1778 when Sir Lionel Lyde, a wealthy tobacco merchant from Bristol, felt obliged to have a new church erected to replace the old one he was demolishing. The leading architect, Nicholas Revett, was called upon and the result was a neo-Classical building, said to have been inspired by the temple of Apollo at Delos. The altar is at the west end, while Sir Lionel is buried in one wing and his wife as far away as possible in the other. Their married life had been full of strife. Look in the churchyard for the grave of Mary Ann South. Despite living to the age of 70, from 1825 to 1895, 'her time was short' was carved on her tombstone. When George Bernard Shaw noted this, he realised that the locals expected longevity, so he decided to settle here.

B In 1906 when he was 50, George Bernard Shaw bought the 'New Rectory', which had been built in 1898. The Irish dramatist, critic and essayist, was already well known for *Man and Superman* (1903). His wife, Charlotte, preferred their London flat at Whitehall Court, but Shaw liked to get away from the crowds. Renaming the house 'Shaw's Corner', he settled down to write *Pygmalion* (1912) and *St Joan* (published in 1924, the year before he was awarded the Nobel Prize for literature). Many famous visitors came here, including the Webbs and the Fabians. Lawrence of Arabia was also a noted guest. Shaw did find longevity here, as he died in 1950 at the age of 94. The last thing he wrote was a *Rhyming Guide to Ayot St Lawrence* which he illustrated with his own photographs. His ashes were scattered in the garden.

'This is my dell, and this my dwelling
Their charm so far beyond my telling
That though in Ireland is my birthplace
This house shall be my final earthplace.'

The property was left to the National Trust and is much as Shaw left it. His hats still hang in the hall, while his pens, dictionaries and typewriter are still on his desk. Shaw liked to write in the study from 10.15 every morning. His typewriter was a portable one and he would take it to the summer house, which is still at the bottom of the garden, when he especially desired peace. He had a bed, a telephone and an electric fire there. Back in the house, Shaw's piano is still in the hall, with a copy of *Messiah* and a book of *Old English Melodies* on it. The piano was kept in the hall so that it could be heard upstairs. Shaw played it loudly during World War II when air raids took place. A keen vegetarian (he wrote to the fledgling Vegan Society in 1944 to state that he ate very few eggs and little dairy produce) Shaw kept fit on a cycling machine, which is also on display. Shaw's Corner is open Apr – Oct. Wed – Sat. 2 – 6, and on Sun & Bank Hol. Mon 12 – 6. Every year in July the Shaw Society commemorates his birthday with a weekend of short plays performed on the lawn of his home.

C Sir Lionel Lyde began to demolish the old church, which dated from the 12th century, in the late 18th century, because it obstructed the view from his new mansion. The Bishop of Lincoln, in whose diocese the parish then was, objected to this and prevented total demolition.

D The manor of Ayot St Lawrence used to belong to the crown. In the 16th century it was occupied by Sir Richard Parr, whose daughter Catherine was one of Henry VIII's six wives. Sir Lionel Lyde built the early Georgian red brick mansion in the 1770s. It was the home of ex-King Michael of Romania during World War II. Later, it became a silk farm which provided the silk for the Prince of Wales' investiture robes.

Over

7 *Turn right with the fence on your right to a gate in the corner of this field and take the track on your right. Ignore a forest path on your left. At the end of the wood, turn left through a gateway. Pass woodland on your right, go right over a stile and bear half left to another stile. Go left down the drive back to Kimpton.*

6 *Cross the bridge over the River Mimram. Pass a farmhouse on your left, then take a gate on your right at the corner where the track bears left. Walk diagonally left across a field to a stile in the fence to the right of a wood.*

5 *Bear right along a lane and go left when the lane veers right. Walk with a hedge on your left down to a road. Continue over a bridge past an old mill on your left and up a lane to pass beds of watercress on your left. Go ahead along a track with trees on your left when the lane forks right. Turn left just before a cottage.*

1 *Start from the church of SS. Peter and Paul in Kimpton. This village is at the junction of the B651 and the B652 5 miles (8 km) east of Luton. It is served by bus nos 44 (Luton-Stevenage), 304 (Hitchin-St Alban's) and 315 (from and to Welwyn Garden City). It is possible to park a car near the church.*
Take the path from the church to the B651, which is the Hitchin Road on the eastern edge of the village. Turn right along this road to its junction with the High Street. Turn left to walk away from the village, keeping to the pavement on the left of the B651. When this route takes the first road on your right (Blackmore End), cross the road carefully and follow the B651, as signposted. When this road bends right, turn left away from it to follow the signposted path.

2 *When you reach a waymark post, veer slightly right across a field, as directed by the yellow arrow. Go ahead over a stile into a wood and keep straight on, ignoring a cross path. Go ahead over a second stile to follow a path to cross a third stile.*

3 *Go ahead out of the wood, with a fence on your right. Look for a stile on your right. Do not cross it, but take the next stile on your right. This leads to what looks like a Greek temple but is, in fact, Ayot St Lawrence's 'new church'. Pass this on your left to reach a road. Bear left to 'Shaw's Corner'. Turn left up a road which bends right past the old church on your left.*

4 *Turn left up the signposted bridleway. Ignore a signposted path on your right and go ahead along a track to pass the manor house on your left.*

Christmashill Wood

B651

Kimpton

B651

Hog Wood

Kimpton Mill

Claggbottom Wood

Ayot House

Church

Ⓓ

Ⓐ

Ⓒ

Ayot St Lawrence

Ⓑ

Shaw's Corner

47

WATTON-AT-STONE
5.5 miles (8.8 km) Easy

0   1 mile

0   1 km

This interesting old village, which can be reached easily by train, is the starting point for a varied walk along clear tracks with extensive views, woodland paths and quiet lanes.

1 *Start from British Rail's station on the London to Stevenage line via Hertford North. Cars can easily be parked in the village of Watton-at-Stone, at the junction of the A119 and A602 between Hertford and Stevenage.*
Go left from the station in the direction of the village and turn left up Hazeldell. Go ahead up a footpath between house nos 27 and 29. Take the road to the right, turn left up a path and go right along the estate road which bends left, then right, to reach the High Street. Turn left to pass a garage on your left and cross the road to The Waggon & Horses on your right. Inspect the stone and turn around to follow the High Street past the garage, now on your right. Continue past a gable with a Union Jack painted on it, on your right. Pass Station Road on your right, noticing the old pump on the corner. Go ahead 50 yards (45 m) and turn right up a signposted path. Turn left at a path junction and pass a sports field on your right, going ahead along a hedged path to the church.

2 *Walk through the churchyard (or take the narrow path to the right of the churchyard hedge). Go left along a lane to a junction and turn right towards Perrywood.*

Watton-at-Stone

Station

Watkin's
Spring North

Church

A602

Perrywood
Farm

Great Gobions
Farm

Bramfield Woods

3 *Go ahead along this lane, past a signposted path to Stapleford on your left and across a bridge over the railway. Pass a signposted path on your right. Pass a house on your left and turn left along a signposted bridleway, with a hedge on your right and extensive views across fields on your left. Reach a lane and turn right. When the lane bears left, turn right through a farmyard.*

4 *Bear left with a field on your right. Go ahead to woods which you pass on your right before entering along a clear track. Fork right along a grassy path preceded by a stile. Ignore side paths and follow the main path as it bends left to a gravel track. Turn right and follow this track when it bends left.*

Over

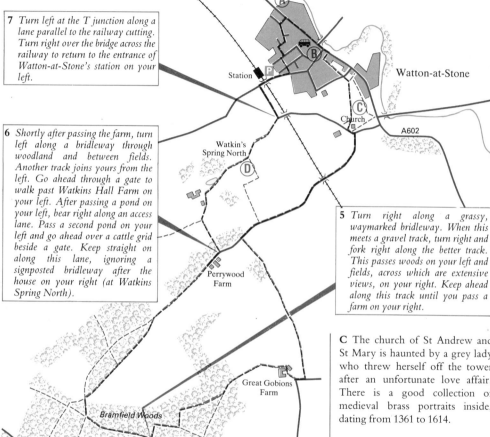

7 *Turn left at the T junction along a lane parallel to the railway cutting. Turn right over the bridge across the railway to return to the entrance of Watton-at-Stone's station on your left.*

6 *Shortly after passing the farm, turn left along a bridleway through woodland and between fields. Another track joins yours from the left. Go ahead through a gate to walk past Watkins Hall Farm on your left. After passing a pond on your left, bear right along an access lane. Pass a second pond on your left and go ahead over a cattle grid beside a gate. Keep straight on along this lane, ignoring a signposted bridleway after the house on your right (at Watkins Spring North).*

5 *Turn right along a grassy, waymarked bridleway. When this meets a gravel track, turn right and fork right along the better track. This passes woods on your left and fields, across which are extensive views, on your right. Keep ahead along this track until you pass a farm on your right.*

C The church of St Andrew and St Mary is haunted by a grey lady who threw herself off the tower after an unfortunate love affair. There is a good collection of medieval brass portraits inside, dating from 1361 to 1614.

D Watkin's Spring North. The name Watton is derived from the Saxon word 'Wat', which means wet or watery. There were natural springs here, including one renowned for its healing properties. People used to travel to Watton-at-Stone to take the waters, but the healing spring has now dried up.

A Watton acquired the suffix 'at-Stone' because of the large rock of Hertfordshire puddingstone which can be seen outside The Waggon & Horses. Watton is an ancient settlement. It was a Roman market place, and Saxons fought Danes here in 1016.

B The canopy over the old pump is a memorial to a soldier who served in Egypt in 1881.

Walk 31

STANDON

3.5 miles (5.6 km) Easy

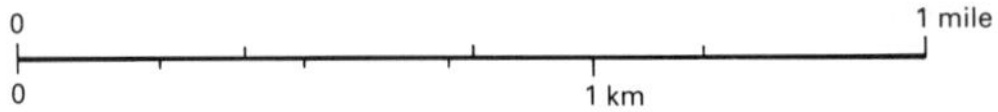

Standon can be reached by bus or car. This walk starts from the bus stop. The young Italian Vincenze Lunardi must have had an excellent view of the River Rib as it winds its way through the valley past 'The Lordship' when he arrived in 1784, completing the first balloon flight in England.

1 *Start from The Heron at the corner of the A120 (Kents Lane) and Station Road in Standon, about 1 mile (1.6 km) east of its junction with the A10. There is a bus stop here for the 331 service between Hertford and Buntingford. Cars can be parked in the village.*
Turn left along the A120 and cross the bridge over the River Rib. Turn right along Stortford Road to pass St Mary's church on your left and continue to a large rock of Hertfordshire puddingstone on a little green on your right.

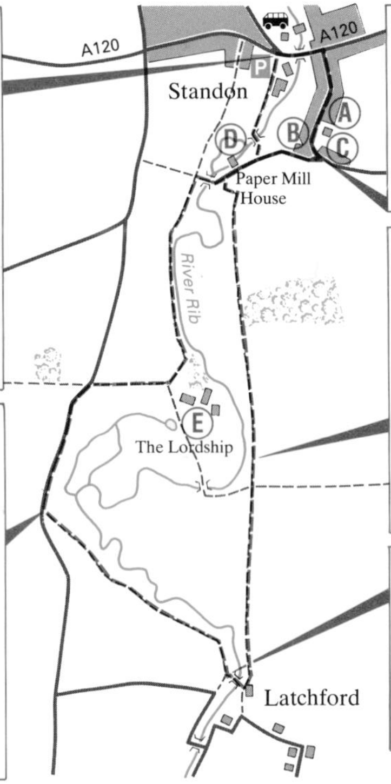

2 *Turn sharply right along Paper Mill Lane. Pass Paper Mill House on your right, before a ford. Just before the ford, turn left along the signposted public bridleway to Latchford. Walk near the fence on your left, with the river away on your right.*

3 *Pass woodland on your left and go ahead through a gate. Continue with a hedge on your left and a view of 'The Lordship' across the river on your right. Bear right near the end of this second meadow and go ahead through a gate. Cross a path and continue walking south. Climb with the hedge on your left, then descend to a gate. Go on to Latchford, where you turn right across a footbridge.*

4 *The right of way crosses the cultivated field on your right. The obviously popular path is along the river bank. With either you turn right and walk with the river on your right. After you pass a small lake, go left through a gate to reach a lane.*

5 *Turn right and follow the lane until a track leads to 'The Lordship' on your right. Turn right along this track but turn left over a stile beside a gate before the house. Walk with the river on your right to a gate. Go through it and turn right across two footbridges. Pass 'Paper Mill House' and turn left up a signposted path. Cross another footbridge and turn right to walk with a hedge on your right to a kissing-gate. Cross the A120 road carefully to return to The Heron and the bus stop.*

(Map labels: A120, Standon, P, A, B, C, Paper Mill House, River Rib, E, The Lordship, Latchford)

A St Mary's church was built by the Knights Hospitaller of St John of Jerusalem. The local lord, Gilbert de Clare, had made the bequest of land to the Order, but the most notable memorial, to the right of the altar, is the tomb of Sir Ralph Sadler. An important Tudor statesman, his monument is guarded by the staff that bore Scotland's flag at the battle of Pinkie, in 1547.

Local gravedigger and sexton, Daniel Clerk is said to be the model for Charles Dickens' gravedigger. He kept old bones in a basket in his cottage. Another notable villager was Richard Gaff who, at the age of 95, married his fifth wife. She bore him five children before he died in 1819.

B This piece of Hertfordshire puddingstone used to stand at the church gate.

C The brick and timber building is the old school, originally a Hospice of the Knights of John.

D 'Paper Mill House' was a water mill making the paper on which bibles were printed.

E 'The Lordship' was the home of Sir Ralph Sadler.

HERTFORD

3 miles (4.8 km) Easy

0   1 mile

0   1 km

Hertford is a very friendly county town, standing where three rivers meet. Its castle was the home of Saxon Kings and the venue for the first Synod of the English church. This walk allows you to explore the castle and to enjoy the 'green finger' that extends into Hertford with the river valleys, including the River Lee Navigation's towpath.

1 *Start from the entrance to the Tourist Office in Hertford Castle. This is in the centre of Hertford, near the St Andrew Street car park, the bus station and the railway station.*
Turn left past the stone which commemorates the holding of the first general synod of the English church here in 673. Bear right to walk with the River Lee on your left and turn left over two footbridges, then bear right over a weir. Turn left over Mill Bridge to Old Cross. Turn right, down a lane (to the right of the library) which leads to the original ford across the river. Return to Old Cross and bear right up Cowbridge. Cross a bridge over the River Beane and take the second road on your right (Port Hill). Pass The Reindeer on your left before turning right into the Warren Meadows.

2 *Follow the path above the River Beane on your right. Go through St Leonard's churchyard. Leave it on your left and turn right.*

3 *Take the gravel track around the churchyard on your right and turn left through a kissing-gate. Go down a path to a footbridge over the river on your right. Cross it and veer left to another bridge, this time over the River Lee. Go across and turn right past Hertford Lock. Follow the towpath to a weir where you switch sides. Pass The Old Barge and turn left over Folly Bridge. Go up Bull Plain. Turn left to 13 Railway Street.*

4 *Turn around and go ahead up Maidenhead Street. Use the pelican crossing to reach the gates of Hertford Castle ahead.*

A Hertford Castle has been in unbroken occupation for nearly one thousand years. The motte of the Norman motte and bailey can be seen, as can the 12th-century curtain wall. The building that is still used is actually the 15th-century gatehouse, altered and extended in the 18th century.

B This is the site of the ford from which Hertford was named.

C The natural amphitheatre of Hartham was the scene of medieval jousting and archery tournaments.

D St Leonard's is the oldest church to survive in Hertford. It has a Saxon font, a leper squint and the remains of an anchorite's cell.

E Hertford Lock is on the Lee Navigation. This is a branch of the River Lee that was widened, deepened and straightened in 1765 to enable barges to reach Hertford.

F Hertford Museum is on your left. It is open Tue – Sat. 10 – 5. Admission is free.

G 13 Railway Street is now occupied by an office of Thomas Cook. It was once the home of Mr Frederick Davis, a musician, and his wife. In March 1899, a man knocked on their door at 3.30am. and asked for an axe so that he could chop a woman's head off. It is not recorded whether one was handed over, but the police were alerted at 3.40am, did nothing for nearly three hours, by which time it was too late. It was a very public murder with plenty of witnesses.

WIDFORD
5.5 miles (8.9 km) Easy

0   1 mile

0   1 km

The part of Hertfordshire that borders Essex is very beautiful. The pretty village of Widford, in particular, was beloved by the essayist Charles Lamb (1775–1834). The sculptor Henry Moore later came to live here. This used to be a fiercely contested border between Saxons and Danes. Now it is a peaceful scene, with some fine beech trees clothing the valley of the River Ash.

2 *Ignoring the footbridge on your left, go ahead over a stile and follow the path with a fence on your right. This is joined by a fence on your left before you reach a lane. Cross this to take a concrete track ahead to the gates of a waterworks. Turn left along a fenced path which soon bends right. Continue along a path called Toto's Way, with a hedge on your left. Cross the B1004 and go up Bourne Lane. Veer left at the traffic barriers on your left to follow the signposted bridleway. Ignore a track going uphill ahead on your right. Follow a lower track ahead on your left. This leads past Mill Wood on your right.*

Perry Green

Hoglands

B

Mill Wood

B1004

River Ash

Hadham Mill

South-end

Nether Street

P

A   Widford

Church

C

B180

1 *Start from The Green Man in Widford. The no 351 bus from Hertford and Bishop's Stortford stops here, and cars can be parked nearby. Widford is at the junction of the B1004 and the B180 about 6 miles (9.7 km) south-west of Bishop's Stortford.*

With your back to The Green Man, turn right and soon fork left. Turn right along Bell Lane, passing a cricket field on your left. Go ahead along Abbott's Lane to the church of St John the Baptist on your right. Turn right to follow a path through the churchyard to *the left of the church. Cross a stile and descend the rough steps. A well-worn path leads to a crossing over a ditch. Go ahead with the River Ash on your left. Reach a footbridge on your left in the far corner of this long meadow. **Do not cross it!***

A The church of St John the Baptist, Widford, contains some very interesting murals, dating back to the 13th century. The most famous grave in the churchyard is that of Mary Field (spelt Feild on

Over

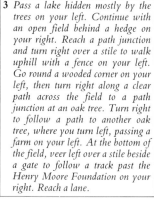

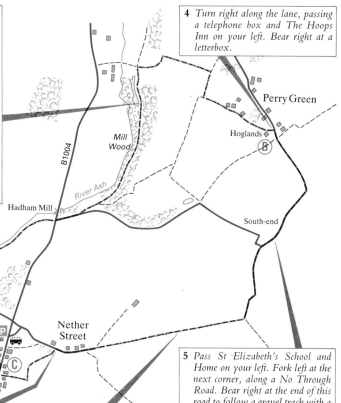

3 *Pass a lake hidden mostly by the trees on your left. Continue with an open field behind a hedge on your right. Reach a path junction and turn right over a stile to walk uphill with a fence on your left. Go round a wooded corner on your left, then turn right along a clear path across the field to a path junction at an oak tree. Turn right to follow a path to another oak tree, where you turn left, passing a farm on your left. At the bottom of the field, veer left over a stile beside a gate to follow a track past the Henry Moore Foundation on your right. Reach a lane.*

4 *Turn right along the lane, passing a telephone box and The Hoops Inn on your left. Bear right at a letterbox.*

5 *Pass St Elizabeth's School and Home on your left. Fork left at the next corner, along a No Through Road. Bear right at the end of this road to follow a gravel track with a hedge on your right. Pass a thatched cottage on your left.*

6 *Continue along a rough track. This becomes a lane. Ignore the first signposted stile on you left, but turn left across the second.*

7 *Cross another stile ahead and bear right. Turn right through a farmyard and turn right along the road back to The Green Man.*

her gravestone). The grandmother of Charles Lamb, she died in 1792 when the essayist was 17. Being the housekeeper at the great house (now demolished) at Blakesware, she was often visited by Charles Lamb, who came to love this area and to know all its inhabitants. 'Kindly hearts have I known,

Kindly hearts they are flown,'

B Henry Moore, the sculptor, came to live here, at 'Hoglands', when his London studio was damaged in 1941. It was still his home when he died in 1986 and now houses the Henry Moore Foundation.

C John Eliot was born in Widford in 1604. He became a Puritan and fled to America, where he mastered the language of the Red Indians in Massachusetts and translated the Bible for them.

53

TRING RESERVOIRS

2 miles (3.2 km) Easy

The navigators (hence *navvy*) who dug the Grand Union Canal at the start of the 19th century little realised that their efforts to produce a means of transport would soon be superseded by the railway, whilst nature would claim the Tring Reservoirs as her territory. Built to store water for the canal, these marl lakes (rich in minerals, plants and fish) are now a National Nature Reserve.

1 *Start from the car park on your right just before the bridge over the Grand Union Canal on the B489 as you go north from Tring.*
The Angler's Retreat is opposite the car park. Go up to the edge of a reservoir and turn to walk with it on your right and the Grand Union Canal down on your left. Go along the canal towpath to a lock.

2 *Retrace your steps from the lock to a path which goes off on your left between two reservoirs. Go ahead to a road.*

3 *Turn right along the road until a stile invites you to turn left. Do so and follow a narrow path through woodland, with the lake on your left. Pass a hide on your left and continue to a stile beside a gate on your right. Cross the stile to follow a lane to a road at a corner with a postbox in the wall.*

4 *Turn right along the road and keep right at a fork. Go right at a second fork to reach a signposted footpath on your left.*

5 *Go through the gap in the hedge on your left to follow the signposted path around the lake (keeping it on your right) until you reach the car park again.*

A The Grand Union Canal links the River Thames in London with Birmingham, Leicester and Nottingham. Tring was on the section known as the Grand Junction Canal, which set new standards of wide locks which, if copied elsewhere, could have lengthened the period of commercial use of the canal system in Britain. A rise of nearly 400 feet (120 m) required the building of many locks, including six known as the Tring Steps. These locks needed a supply of water to supply the upper level of the canal, so four reservoirs were dug. Fed by natural springs, they are marl lakes, found only in chalk or limestone areas. The minerals in the water have led to an abundance of plants and fish.

B Marsworth Reservoir is famous for its wildfowl, which were the chief reason for Tring Reservoirs being designated as a National Nature Reserve in 1955. You can normally see tufted duck (black crests and white flanks), pochard (chestnut-red heads), mallard and shoveler. Teal, wigeon, gadwall, greylag goose and goldeneye also visit. One of the most splendid birds to come is the goosander, a fish-eating duck with a bottle-green head and a rosy-pink body. Coots and dabchicks are also present, while bitterns winter here sometimes. The great crested grebe can also be seen here. Between December and May you may see their courtship display. Indeed the biologist and writer Sir Julian Huxley came here to study them. Herons nest in the trees at the back of the Marsworth Reservoir and the reedbeds contain a large colony of reed warblers. These birds return here annually, migrating from Africa.

C Tringford Reservoir has much richer vegetation on its bank. You may see woodpeckers in the trees. Migrant wading birds, such as green and common sandpipers, can be seen from the hide.

D The pumping station which controls the flow of water into the canal is on your left.

THE COLE GREEN WAY

2.5 miles (4 km) Easy

0 —————————————— 1 mile
0 —————————————— 1 km

Disused railway lines can be turned into assets for walkers and naturalists. Hertfordshire County Council realised this and you can now enjoy a gentle stroll along part of their Cole Green Way. Each season provides something of interest, from the wild pansies of spring to the scarlet pimpernel of summer, the blackberries of autumn and the winter heliotrope.

3 *Go up the waymarked path to a lane and turn left along it. Pass a farm on your right and turn left along a signposted path to Roxford. This follows a hedge around on your left to a patch of woodland. Turn right over a stile into the corner of a field.*

2 *Cross the bridge over the road and follow the dismantled railway for nearly 1 mile (1.6 km).*

1 *The start of this walk is near Hertingfordbury, which is on the south-western outskirts of Hertford. Take the road (St Mary's Lane) south through the village, passing Hertingfordbury's church on your left. Go under a bridge to find the car park from which this walk starts on your left. Go up steps in the old railway embankment to reach the Cole Green Way and turn left along it.*

To Hertfordingbury

Ⓐ Cole Green Way

Southfield Wood

Ⓑ

East End Green

6 *Turn left through a signposted gate to follow a path above a farm on your right. Go ahead along a narrow fenced path parallel to a farm track below. Go through a gate and veer slightly left along a narrow hedged path. Go ahead through woodland and continue with an open field on your left and a hedge on your right, then with trees on your left and a field on your right. When you reach St Mary's Lane turn left along it back to the car park on your right, just before the bridge.*

4 *Go ahead with a hedge on your left. Turn left along the waymarked path at the end of the field, soon passing a wood on your right.*

5 *Bear right around the wood to a stile beside a gate in the corner of the field. Continue down a field with a hedge on your left.*

A The Cole Green Way utilises the now dismantled railway line which once connected Hertford with Welwyn Garden City. It was opened in 1858 and closed to passengers in 1951. Goods services continued until 1962. Cole Green is a hamlet on the old railway approximately half-way between Hertford and Welwyn Garden City. In 1974 Hertfordshire County Council acquired the section of the line from Hertford to its junction with the A414 near Cole Green. It was opened as a route for walkers, riders and cyclists and called The Cole Green Way. The banks which used to be cut or burnt by the railway in order to prevent the growth of scrub and tall herbs are now allowed to develop naturally as a wildlife habitat. Several layers of vegetation can be discerned. Tall oak and ash trees grow on the edge of the banks, with the scrubland area on the banks containing hawthorn, sloe, brambles and wild roses. Small wild flowers, such as coltsfoot, ox-eye daisies and blue vetches grow on the grass edges, while lichens and mosses prefer the ballast of the track bed. Insects, small mammals and birds all find this an attractive environment, with the brimstone, red admiral and the colourful peacock butterflies evident from mid April.

B Green woodpeckers may be heard in these woods.

BERKHAMSTED
5.3 miles (8.5 km) Easy

Berkhamsted's thickly wooded common makes this a particularly pleasant walk. Such woodland is reminiscent of the Middle Ages and it seems appropriate to come across the ruins of a once great castle. Berkhamsted is now better known for its public school, which was attended by Graham Greene, the novelist.

A The Saxons submitted to William the Conqueror in December 1066, two months after the battle of Hastings, at Berkhamsted Castle. William's coronation, in London, followed on Christmas Day, and he gave Berkhamsted to his half-brother, Robert of Mortain. Later, it became the home of Thomas á Becket when he was Lord Chancellor. King John gave it to his Queen Isabella, but the French helped the English barons to take it from her in 1216. Henry III gave it to his brother Richard, Earl of Cornwall, whose marriage to the queen's sister was celebrated here with a great banquet.

Edward II's favourite, Piers Gaveston, owned the castle from 1308 to 1309 and held another historic banquet here when he married the king's niece. Edward III restored the castle for the Black Prince, and King John of France was kept a prisoner here after Poitiers, in 1356. Chaucer was clerk of the works here in the reign of Richard II. Edward IV gave the castle to his mother, who died here. Three of Henry VIII's six queens lived in the castle – Catharine of Aragon, Anne Boleyn and Jane Seymour, and they let the place fall into decay. Its stones were subsequently taken for building material by Sir Edward Cary in Elizabeth I's time. Today there are just the very impressive earthworks and a little ragged walling left of the castle, which is right next to the railway that was built in 1838. A green lawn now marks the site of the outer court, surrounded by a deep bank and ditch. A fine conical mound is in the north-east corner. The old Norman well is within the circular low walling of the keep. Another bank and ditch surround the inner earthworks, while a third bank lies on the north and east sides, strengthened by great bastions of earth.

B The place-name Coldharbour is associated with ley, or earth energy, lines. It recalls the shelter of the Cole Man, or surveyor. Coldharbour does not refer to a cold place. Quite often, it is spelt Coleharbour or Cole Harbour, as in the old jingle recorded by Alfred Watkins:
'Silver John is dead and gone
And buried in Cole Harbour'.
The Welsh word coel is derived from gole, meaning light or splendour. Our word coal may also be derived from this.

C The ancient Beorchehamstede was a settlement on the old Roman Akeman Street. It is most famous today for its grammar school, which was founded by John Incent, the Dean of St Paul's, in the 16th century. The church is one of the biggest in the county. Inside is the tomb of John Sayer, chief cook of Charles II, who lived at Berkhamsted Place and founded a row of almshouses at the west end of the town. One of the rectors here was the father of the poet William Cowper, who was born in a now demolished rectory in 1731. Nothing was too homely for Cowper's pen. Anticipating Wordsworth, he found his poetry in the fieldpaths and lanes, rather than in the libraries and rules of conventional contemporaries, such as Pope. Cowper wrote about his birthplace:
'Where once we dwelt our name is heard no more,
Children not thine have trod my nursery floor'.
Cowper was to write his finest poetry, including a poem on Boadicea, at the home of the Unwins in Huntingdon. When Mary Unwin became a widow, she nursed Cowper through nervous breakdowns. Her own health suffered, she died, then he wrote a final poem and died too.

Over

3 Turn half left to enter the corner of the next field, with woodland behind the fence on your left. Go ahead to cross a stile beside a gate in the next corner. Descend with the fence on your left. Go left over

a stile into a nature reserve and follow the path to a stile in the corner of a field. Go ahead with a hedge on your left, crossing a stile on the way to a stile giving access to woodland.

4 Go ahead 20 yards (18 m), then bear left along a woodland path. Join a track coming from your right and go ahead to Coldharbour Farm. Stop here and turn around to retrace your steps along the track but fork left towards an open field and bear left with the edge of the wood on your left. The path goes ahead through trees to reach a road.

5 Turn right to follow a path back into the trees. Continue with trees on your left and an open field on your right. When the track bends right, go ahead into the trees. Maintain your direction along a forest path. To the left of its start is a notice about pollarded trees. Ignore all side paths and go ahead uphill to pass a second notice about old pollarded trees. Your path becomes a narrower woodland path but goes on to reach a stile at the edge of the forest.

6 Bear left, with the hedge on your left, to a stile beside a gate. Go ahead, switching the hedge to your right after passing a farm on your left. Pass between cricket fields to reach Castle Hill and retrace your steps to the station.

1 Start from Berkhamsted's station on British Rail's Euston to Northampton line. Cars can be parked here.
Leave by the northern exit to go up Brownlow Road. The ruins of the castle are on your right. When Brownlow Road bends right, go straight ahead up Castle Hill and bear left uphill with this road. At the top of the hill, bear right along a signposted footpath, soon forking right to pass Castle Hill Farm on your left.

2 Go ahead over a stile beside a gate to walk with a hedge on your left. Pass a stile on your left then cross a stile beside a gate ahead. Continue with a fence on your left and a hedge on your right. Turn right over a stile at a path junction and walk with a hedge on your left. Bear right with this path, beside trees.

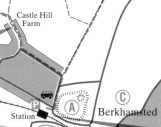

Walk 37
HEMEL HEMPSTEAD
5 miles (8 km) Moderate

```
0                                    1 mile
|----|----|----|----|----|----|
0                1 km
```

This walk leaves the railway station to follow what is probably the most picturesque section of the Grand Union Canal as it crosses the Chilterns. A climb up the Westbrook Hay golf course brings fine views of the Bulbourne valley. A rural plateau leads to Felden, where the path descends through the trees to reach the southern edge of Hemel Hempstead, with its railway station.

3 Turn right along the pavement of the A41 for 350 yards (320 m). Just before the village hall at Bourne End, turn left to cross the road carefully and go up a signposted bridleway. Go ahead over a stile beside a gate to walk with a hedge on your right, keeping a watch for flying golf balls.

2 Pass under a small roadbridge. Continue with the quiet of the canal on your right and the roar of trains on your left. Go under the railway to walk with a lake behind the fence on your left. Pass Kenby International Boat Yard on your right and turn left opposite The Three Horseshoes. Follow a lane to the A41 road.

1 Start from Hemel Hempstead's station on British Rail's line between Euston and Northampton. Cars can be parked here.
Go left from the station entrance to a roundabout and turn right along the road which goes over a bridge across a canal. Turn left to follow the towpath with the canal on your right.

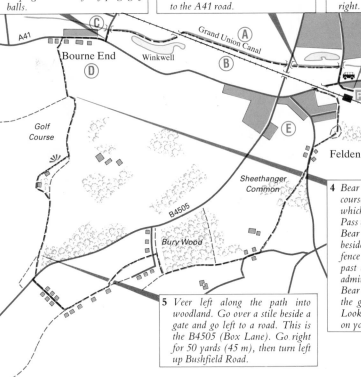

4 Bear left at the edge of the golf course to follow a signposted path which soon bears right, uphill. Pass a clump of trees on your right. Bear right at the third signpost, beside an oak tree, to walk with a fence on your left. Follow the track past a bungalow on your left and admire the fine view on your right. Bear left to follow the drive past the golf clubhouse on your right. Look for a public footpath signpost on your left after the car park.

5 Veer left along the path into woodland. Go over a stile beside a gate and go left to a road. This is the B4505 (Box Lane). Go right for 50 yards (45 m), then turn left up Bushfield Road.

Over

58

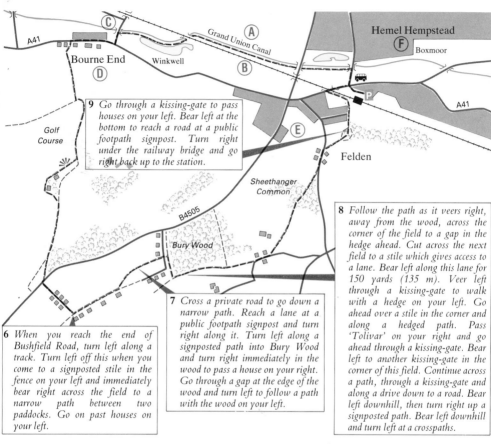

9 Go through a kissing-gate to pass houses on your left. Bear left at the bottom to reach a road at a public footpath signpost. Turn right under the railway bridge and go right back up to the station.

8 Follow the path as it veers right, away from the wood, across the corner of the field to a gap in the hedge ahead. Cut across the next field to a stile which gives access to a lane. Bear left along this lane for 150 yards (135 m). Veer left through a kissing-gate to walk with a hedge on your left. Go ahead over a stile in the corner and along a hedged path. Pass 'Tolivar' on your right and go ahead through a kissing-gate. Bear left to another kissing-gate in the corner of this field. Continue across a path, through a kissing-gate and along a drive down to a road. Bear left downhill, then turn right up a signposted path. Bear left downhill and turn left at a crosspaths.

7 Cross a private road to go down a narrow path. Reach a lane at a public footpath signpost and turn right along it. Turn left along a signposted path into Bury Wood and turn right immediately in the wood to pass a house on your right. Go through a gap at the edge of the wood and turn left to follow a path with the wood on your left.

6 When you reach the end of Bushfield Road, turn left along a track. Turn left off this when you come to a signposted stile in the fence on your left and immediately bear right across the field to a narrow path between two paddocks. Go on past houses on your left.

A This is the Grand Union Canal, which links London with the Midlands. The little River Bulbourne keeps it company here. The chalk springs of the Chilterns were once famous for their watercress beds, but trout farming has now taken over. You pass Boxmoor Top Lock.

B Trains roar past on this electrified mainline between London Euston and Birmingham, Liverpool, Manchester and Glasgow.

C By Winkwell Swing Bridge is The Three Horseshoes Inn, which dates back to 1535, nearly 300 years before the canal was built.

D William Cobbett noted that 'the country children never looked better clad, cleaner or fatter' than they did at Bourne End.

E A Roman villa was sited here.

F Hemel Hempstead is one of Hertfordshire's new towns.

VERULAMIUM

7.5 miles (12 km) Easy

Try to allow a whole day for this walk. The route is not a problem, indeed half of it follows a private road which is open to walkers except on one token day of the year (May 1st). It is time that will be at a premium if you visit all the places along the way. It is not difficult to get to St Albans, whether by train, bus or car, and the cathedral can be found easily.

2 Reach St Michael's Street, and have a look at Kingsbury Water Mill across the road on your right. Turn left to go along St Michael's Street, noticing the Verulamium Museum in the corner on your left, opposite St Michael's church. Both places are worth a visit. Continue along St Michael's Street to the A4147, where there is a pelican crossing. Cross to the 'private road' opposite.

1 There are two British Rail stations in St Albans, numerous bus services, and plenty of signposted car parks. Start from St Albans Cathedral's Chapter House and Visitors' Centre on the south side of the cathedral. With the Chapter House at your back, turn half-right to follow a footpath diagonally down towards the River Ver. Pass Ye Olde Fighting Cocks on your right, go across a bridge on your left and turn right to follow a path between a lake on your left and the River Ver on your right.

3 Go ahead along this estate lane, passing the Roman theatre on your left. Keep to the estate lane, ignoring the waymarked 'Ver Walk' on your right. Pass Maynes Farm and ignore a track opposite it. When the estate lane forks just before Gorhambury, go right to pass the house on your left. Bear left with the lane, then right to pass the ruins of Old Gorhambury on your right.

Old Gorhambury

Gorhambury

(F)

(G) (H)

(E)

(B)

(D) (C)

Stud Cottages

Prae Wood

(I) (J)

Cathedral

(A)

St Alban's

Hill End Farm

A4147

M10

Park Wood

M1

Potters Crouch

4 Pass 'Temple Cottage' on your left and bear left downhill. Turn right to pass Stud Cottages on your right and follow a rough track which becomes a concrete track up to Hill End Farm. Continue under the M10 and emerge on the A4147. Cross this road carefully to go ahead along Appspond Lane, with the M1 on your right.

5 Turn left at Potters Crouch and fork right at The Holly Bush. Walk with a forest on your left, passing a lane on your right. Turn left along a signposted footpath, walking with the forest on your left to a stile ahead. Go ahead over a footbridge across the M10. Cross another stile and follow the path around trees on your left before turning right to cross a field towards St Alban's.

6 Follow the path across a grassy area on your left, then bear right up a narrow path between houses. Maintain your direction, crossing three estate roads. Pass a cricket field on your right, go ahead across a road at a pelican crossing and follow the footpath ahead beside the Roman wall. Pass the lake on your left and retrace your steps from Ye Olde Fighting Cocks.

Over

The Cathedral, St Albans

A The cathedral and abbey church of St Alban was built on the spot where Alban, England's first Christian martyr, was executed in 209, when Severns was Roman emperor. St Albans, the most Romanised part of Britain, later became part of the territory of Offa, king of the Mercians, who founded the abbey in 793, the old Roman town providing the building materials. The present building was begun by the Normans in 1077. The abbey was dissolved in 1539 but the building was bought by the local people to serve as their parish church. It fell into decay and was restored by Lord Grimthorpe in the mid 19th century. It became a cathedral – the second largest cathedral in Britain – in 1877.

B Kingsbury Water Mill is a fully restored and working 16th-century mill. It occupies the site of a mill mentioned in the Domesday Book and is open Wed – Sat 11 – 6, and Sun 12 – 6 (5 in winter).

C Verulamium Museum is open Mon – Sat 10 – 5.30, and Sun 2 – 5.30. It contains a large number of finds from the Roman town, including good mosaics.

D St Michael's church covers the Roman basilica (town hall) and forum (market place).

E This is the only visible Roman theatre in Britain.

F Gorhambury was built in the late 18th century. It contains paintings of the Bacon family and is open to the public on Thursday afternoons from May to September.

G Old Gorhambury, now a ruin, was the family home of Sir Francis Bacon. A genius, he is thought by some to be the true author of Shakespeare's plays.

H Temple Cottages were built in the mid 18th century as a Palladian-style garden temple.

I Verulamium's Roman wall was built about AD200.

J The south-east, or London, gate was where Watling Street entered the city from the south.

LITTLE BERKHAMSTED

6 miles (9.7 km) Easy

When this walk passes Little Berkhamsted, you are near the birthplace of Tom Ken, who became a bishop and wrote the hymn:

'Awake, my soul, and with the sun Thy daily stage of duty run.'
The beauty of this area would stir even the most lethargic of souls. Recent inhabitants of Little Berkhamsted include the pop stars Donovan and Adam Ant. Cricket commentator Brian Johnson was born here.

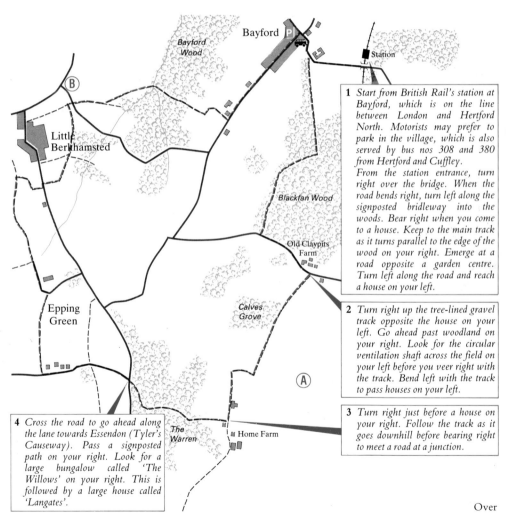

1 *Start from British Rail's station at Bayford, which is on the line between London and Hertford North. Motorists may prefer to park in the village, which is also served by bus nos 308 and 380 from Hertford and Cuffley.*
From the station entrance, turn right over the bridge. When the road bends right, turn left along the signposted bridleway into the woods. Bear right when you come to a house. Keep to the main track as it turns parallel to the edge of the wood on your right. Emerge at a road opposite a garden centre. Turn left along the road and reach a house on your left.

2 *Turn right up the tree-lined gravel track opposite the house on your left. Go ahead past woodland on your right. Look for the circular ventilation shaft across the field on your left before you veer right with the track. Bend left with the track to pass houses on your left.*

3 *Turn right just before a house on your right. Follow the track as it goes downhill before bearing right to meet a road at a junction.*

4 *Cross the road to go ahead along the lane towards Essendon (Tyler's Causeway). Pass a signposted path on your right. Look for a large bungalow called 'The Willows' on your right. This is followed by a large house called 'Langates'.*

Over

62

0   1 mile

0   1 km

6 When the track bends right, go ahead along a woodland path. Go through a gate and turn sharply right to a stile in the corner of the field. Cross the next field to another stile, to be crossed **with care** as it gives access onto a road. Go ahead through the gate opposite to walk with a hedge on your right. Follow the path as it veers left beside a fence on your right. Notice the folly ahead. Turn right over a stile in the corner of the field and turn left to follow a path into woodland. Emerge to walk with a hedge on your right, crossing a stile ahead into a second field. Turn right at the end of this to reach a lane.

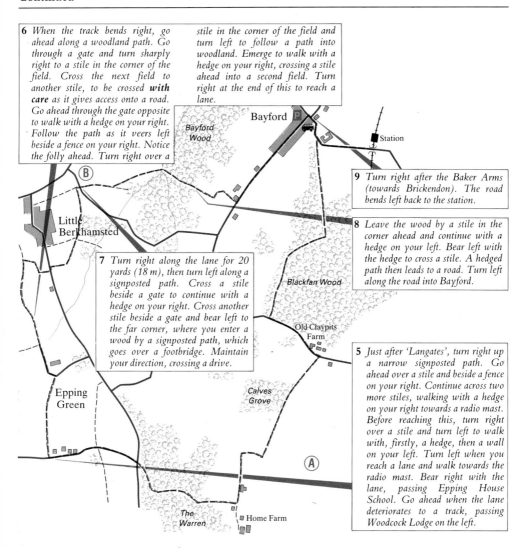

9 Turn right after the Baker Arms (towards Brickendon). The road bends left back to the station.

8 Leave the wood by a stile in the corner ahead and continue with a hedge on your left. Bear left with the hedge to cross a stile. A hedged path then leads to a road. Turn left along the road into Bayford.

7 Turn right along the lane for 20 yards (18 m), then turn left along a signposted path. Cross a stile beside a gate to continue with a hedge on your right. Cross another stile beside a gate and bear left to the far corner, where you enter a wood by a signposted path, which goes over a footbridge. Maintain your direction, crossing a drive.

5 Just after 'Langates', turn right up a narrow signposted path. Go ahead over a stile and beside a fence on your right. Continue across two more stiles, walking with a hedge on your right towards a radio mast. Before reaching this, turn right over a stile and turn left to walk with, firstly, a hedge, then a wall on your left. Turn left when you reach a lane and walk towards the radio mast. Bear right with the lane, passing Epping House School. Go ahead when the lane deteriorates to a track, passing Woodcock Lodge on the left.

A The protrusion in the field on your left is a circular ventilation shaft from the Ponsbourne railway tunnel.

B The red tower is a folly built in the 17th century by John Stratton. It was supposed to enable him to see his ships anchored in the Thames. Later, it was made into an observatory. Tom Ken, who became Bishop of Bath and Wells, was born nearby in 1637.

RICKMANSWORTH

5 miles (8 km) Moderate

This walk takes you to the very edge of London, although green fields and woodland (brightened by bluebells in May) are the chief attractions. Of course, such countryside so close to London is in great demand and the outward route is shared with golfers.

1 *Start from Rickmansworth station. This is on London Underground's Metropolitan line and on British Rail's Marylebone – Aylesbury line. Many London buses also stop here, and cars can be parked opposite.*
With your back to the station entrance, turn right and go right again under the railway bridge. Turn left along the High Street and turn right, up the bollarded-off Bury Street. Bend left with Bury Street to reach Church Street and turn right. Cut through the churchyard ahead and cross the road to pass a roundabout on your right. Go ahead across bridges, passing a canal lock on your left. Curve left along the A4145, ignoring the A404 on your right. Continue along Moor Lane for a few yards, then take the drive signposted 'Moor Park Mansion' on your right. After 20 yards (18 m), veer right over a stile to follow a public footpath up the golf course (watch out for golf balls).

2 *The footpath cuts straight across the grass to cross the drive near the clubhouse. Continue up a track just to the right of the professional's shop. Aim for the far right corner of the golf course, crossing the drive again and passing the mansion on your left. White arrows mark the way.*

5 *Reach a London Borough of Hillingdon sign. Turn sharply right along a signposted path which goes over waymarked stiles. Reach a lane and go left for 300 yards (270 m). Turn right over a stile, then turn left along a path over waymarked stiles. Turn left to reach Sherfield Avenue. At its end, go right to The White Bear. Retrace your steps to the start.*

4 *Turn half right across the field, passing woodland on your left. Go ahead through a waymarked gap and over a stile in the next hedge. Follow an enclosed path to a lane and turn left. Pass The Rose & Crown and turn right.*

3 *Follow the waymarked path to the right of a white house. This leads to the A404. Turn right along the pavement. Pass Home Farm Road on your right and cross to 'Primrose Lodge' on your left. Turn left down a signposted path. Turn right over a stile and turn left at once to walk down to cross a stile ahead. Go on with the hedge on your left. Turn left across a waymarked stile.*

A Batchworth Lock is an attractive feature of the Grand Union Canal, which links London and Birmingham.

B Moor Park Mansion is now leased to the golf club by the district council. Built in 1678 for the Duke of Monmouth, it was rebuilt in the Palladian style in 1720 by Benjamin Styles.

BARTHOLOMEW WALKS SERIES

Designed to meet the requirements of both experienced and inexperienced walkers, the guides in this series are ideal for anyone who enjoys exploring on foot. They describe the best routes across our greatest walking country from Inverness to the New Forest and Cork & Kerry.

● In each guide, there are at least 30 carefully chosen, easy-to-follow walks over rights of way, with detailed route descriptions accompanying special maps.

● Country walks are graded according to distance and terrain and start from a convenient parking area. The route always returns to the car park, usually by a circular walk and, where appropriate, access by public transport is also possible.

● Notes on local history, geography and wildlife add interest to the walks and the unique notebook format is especially easy to use.

EXPLORE THE BROADS
0 7028 0772 9   £3·50

WALK CORK & KERRY
0 7028 0949 7   £4·95

WALK THE CORNISH COASTAL PATH
A special format step-by-step guide to the entire length of the Cornish Coastal Path (Marsland Mouth - Cremyll).
0 7028 0902 0   £4·95

WALK THE COTSWOLDS
0 7028 0908 X   £4·95

WALK THE DALES
0 7028 0800 8   £4·95

MORE WALKS IN THE DALES
0 7028 0948 9   £4·95

YORKSHIRE DALES VISITOR'S PACK
Containing a copy of *Walk the Dales* and a folded 1 inch map of the Yorkshire Dales in a clear, plastic carrying wallet.
0 7028 0932 2   £6·95

WALK DARTMOOR
0 7028 0688 9   £3·95

WALK DORSET & HARDY'S WESSEX
0 7028 0906 3   £3·95

WALK EXMOOR & THE QUANTOCKS
0 7028 0910 1   £3·95

WALK HERTS & BUCKS
0 7028 0953 5   £4·95

WALK THE LAKES
0 7028 8111 2   £3·95

MORE WALKS IN THE LAKES
0 7028 0819 9   £4·95

LAKE DISTRICT WALKING PACK
Containing a copy of *Walk the Lakes* and a folded 1 inch map of the Lake District in a clear, plastic carrying wallet.
0 7028 0876 8   £6·95

WALK LOCH LOMOND
& THE TROSSACHS
0 7028 0744 3   £4·95

WALK LOCH NESS & THE RIVER SPEY
0 7028 0787 7   £3·95

BARTHOLOMEW WALKS SERIES (Contd)

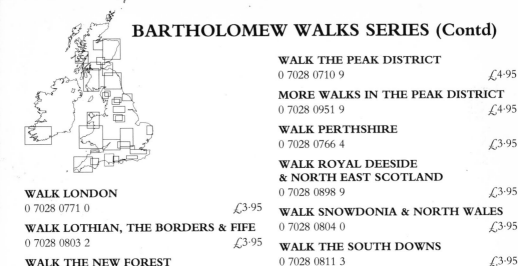

WALK THE PEAK DISTRICT
0 7028 0710 9 £4·95

MORE WALKS IN THE PEAK DISTRICT
0 7028 0951 9 £4·95

WALK PERTHSHIRE
0 7028 0766 4 £3·95

**WALK ROYAL DEESIDE
& NORTH EAST SCOTLAND**
0 7028 0898 9 £3·95

WALK SNOWDONIA & NORTH WALES
0 7028 0804 0 £3·95

WALK THE SOUTH DOWNS
0 7028 0811 3 £3·95

WALK THE SOUTH PENNINES
0 7028 0955 1 £4·95

**WALK SOUTH WALES
& THE WYE VALLEY**
0 7028 0904 7 £3·95

WALK SOUTH WEST SCOTLAND
0 7028 0900 4 £3·95

WALK THE THAMES & CHILTERNS
0 7028 0802 4 £3·95

WALK LONDON
0 7028 0771 0 £3·95

WALK LOTHIAN, THE BORDERS & FIFE
0 7028 0803 2 £3·95

WALK THE NEW FOREST
0 7028 0810 5 £4·95

WALK THE NORTH DOWNS
0 7028 0742 7 £3·95

WALK THE NORTH YORK MOORS
0 7028 0743 5 £3·95

WALK NORTHUMBRIA
0 7028 0959 4 £4·95

WALK OBAN, MULL & LOCHABER
0 7028 0801 6 £3·95

Guides in this series may be purchased from good bookshops. In the event of difficulty copies may be obtained by post. *Please send your order with your remittance to*
**BARTHOLOMEW BOOKSERVICE BY POST,
PO BOX 29, DOUGLAS, ISLE OF MAN, BRITISH ISLES.**

NAME _____

ADDRESS _____

_____

_____

Please enclose a cheque or postal order made out to 'Bartholomew' for the amount due and allow 25 pence per book postage & packing fee up to a maximum of £3.00.
While every effort is made to keep prices low, it is sometimes necessary to increase cover prices at short notice.
Bartholomew reserves the right to show new retail prices on covers which may differ from those previously advertised in the text or elsewhere.